A BRIEF HISTORY OF
ROCKVILLE CENTRE

A BRIEF HISTORY OF
ROCKVILLE CENTRE

The Heritage and History of a Village

MARILYN NUNES DEVLIN

THE History PRESS

Published by The History Press
Charleston, SC 29403
www.historypress.net

Unless otherwise noted, all images are from the archives of the Museum of the Village of Rockville Centre.

First published 2011
Manufactured in the United States

ISBN 978.1.60949.138.3

Library of Congress Cataloging-in-Publication Data
Devlin, Marilyn Nunes.
Brief history of Rockville Centre : the heritage and history of a village / Marilyn Nunes Devlin.
p. cm.
Includes index.
ISBN 978-1-60949-138-3
1. Rockville Centre (N.Y.)--History. 2. Rockville Centre (N.Y.)--Biography. 3. Rockville Centre (N.Y.)--Social life and customs. 4. New York Region--History, Local. I. Title.
F129.R81D48 2011
974.7'245--dc23
2011032147

Notice: The information in this book is true and complete to the best of our knowledge. It is offered without guarantee on the part of the author or The History Press. The author and The History Press disclaim all liability in connection with the use of this book.

This book is dedicated to the memory of Margaret Phelps Hopkins, who created the Historical Research Archive at the Museum of the Village of Rockville Centre.

CONTENTS

ACKNOWLEDGEMENTS

A great big thank-you to all the people and organizations who helped make this book possible. Their contributions, encouragement, time and thoughtfulness are much appreciated. Specifically, thank you to:

The Board of Trustees of the Museum of the Village of Rockville Centre for the use of the Phillips House as a research and writing space; The History Press, especially my editor, Whitney Tarella for her guidance, understanding and hand-holding throughout this wonderful experience; Lorraine Jackson, from Molloy College's Technical Services, for agreeing to scan all the images used in this book; the Nassau County Photographic Archive; Alene Scoblete, archivist at the Rockville Centre Public Library; Polly Vanich; Patricia Odermatt; Laura and James Hennig; our good friends Charles and Nellie Huttunen; and last but never least, my husband, Bill, without whose encouragement and cheering all would be lost, and for keeping everything running smoothly on the homefront.

Chapter 1

A RIVER RUNS THROUGH IT

Through the Great South Woods, where wolves still roamed, flowed the crystal clear water and swift current of Mill River. Along its banks stood the farms and homesteads of several hearty pioneer families. Realizing they resided within an ecological environment of great economic value, they began to create a milling industry that would continue to prosper over the next two centuries.

One of these entrepreneurial pioneers was Michael DeMott. Using fill from a nearby sand hole, he began work on his mill, dam and pond in 1710. Twenty years later, he turned over ownership to Anthony DeMott, owner of a large tract of land extending as far north as present-day Southern State Parkway and bounded on the east by Grand Avenue in Baldwin, on the west by Hempstead Lake State Park and on the south by Merrick Road, then known as South Country Road.

Anthony DeMott married Phoebe Bedell in St. George's Episcopal Church in Hempstead on July 27, 1747. They built their homestead facing south to catch the sun at right angles to the road. Indicative of its early origins, its gable roof, two interior chimneys and symmetrical front

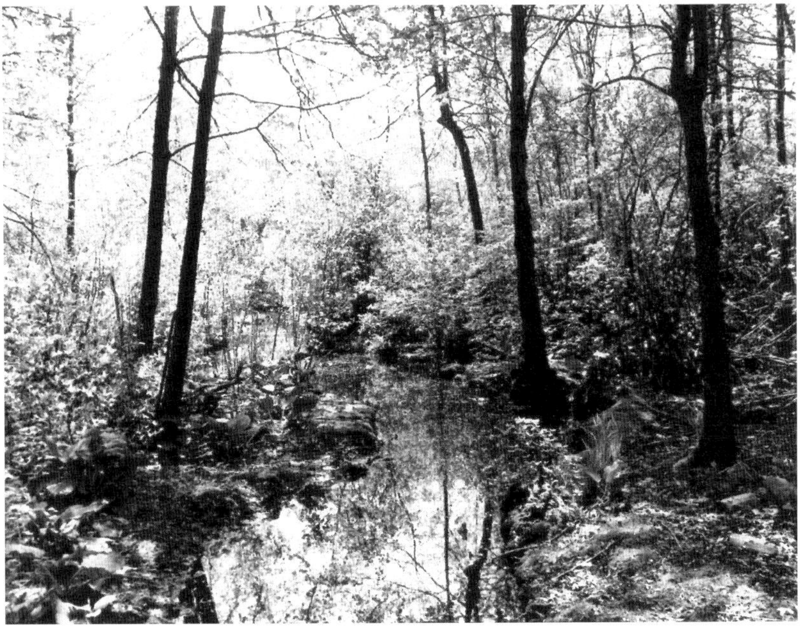

Above: The Great South Woods surrounding Mill River and the small community inhabited by the pioneering families of what would become Rockville Centre.

Below: Mill River, along which stood the six mills built to start what would become a very economically viable milling industry.

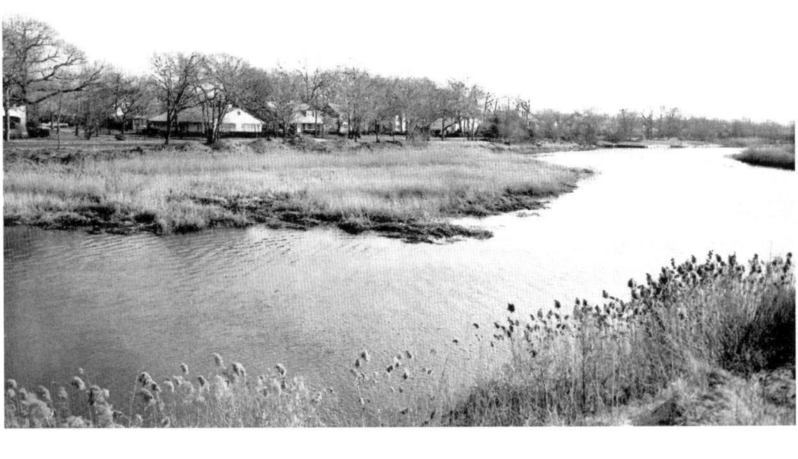

elevation spoke to the orderliness of the eighteenth-century aesthetic. Their home still stands at Hempstead Avenue and Cash Lane, although there have been many additions and subtractions made.

The Revolutionary War intruded on life along Mill River in 1776, when a skirmish took place at DeMott's Mill between the Loyalists and the rebels. To escape Washington's army, a band of Tories hid out in the swamp near the mill. DeMott, being a Loyalist, would hang a sheet out the window to warn of impending danger. A party of Whig soldiers made their way to the mill in sedge boats. One of the party, Stephen Rider, climbed a tree to reconnoiter, when a musket ball whizzed by his head. Seeing smoke from whence it came, he fired a shot that passed through the body of George Smith. The wound was treated by a Dr. Searing, and the first blood was spilled on Long Island in the War for Independence.

After retiring from the mill, Anthony DeMott resumed farming his land. Three times a week, in the heart of the growing season, he took the journey into the Wallabout

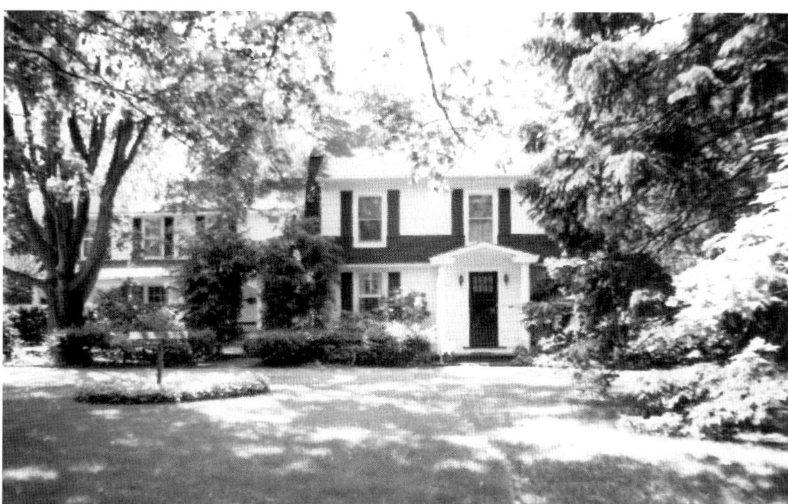

The home of Anthony and Phoebe DeMott, as it looks today, was originally built in 1749 at the corner of Hempstead Avenue and Cash Lane.

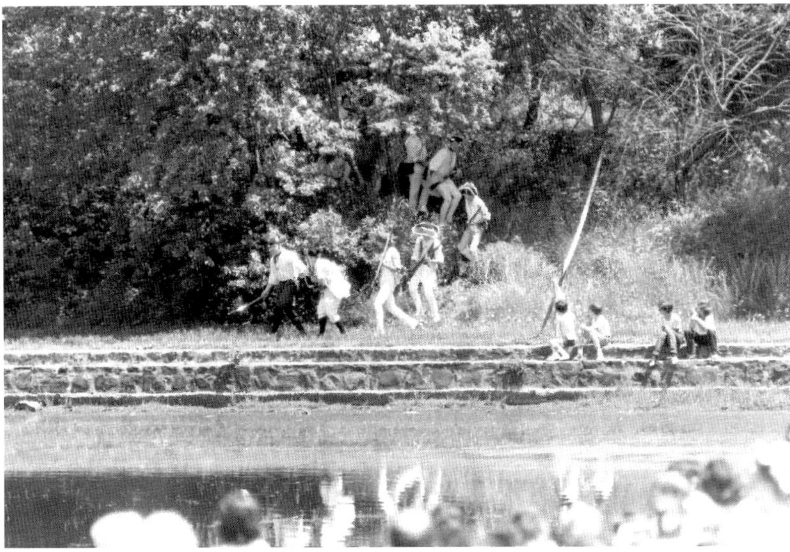

A 1976 reenactment of the skirmish at DeMott's Mill, circa 1776, where the first blood was shed on Long Island during the Revolutionary War.

Market in Brooklyn to sell his produce. Along with his four children, DeMott established a family legacy that dominated Rockville Centre life well into the twentieth century.

By the early 1800s, Mordecai Rock Smith had taken over ownership and operation of the mill that his father, Israel, had purchased from DeMott in 1780. Renamed Smith's Mill and Pond, it no longer was just a gristmill; it now housed carding and fulling machines and a general store. Smith's Pond can still be seen just north of Merrick Road.

Both religious and social life in this small yet growing hamlet centered on the nondenominational Sand Hole Episcopal Methodist Church. Built on land donated by Isaac Denton and raised by the residents, it opened its doors in 1790. Soon it was being used by Methodist circuit riders. With more families of the Methodist faith moving to the area, the church became solely the Sand Hole Methodist Church.

Hardships were many for these hearty pioneers. In 1816, the frost lasted into the fall in what became known as the year without a summer. The crops never ripened, and there was no grist for the six mills now dotting the banks of Mill River. With little time to recover from this economic devastation, a hurricane hit the south shore of Long Island, raising the tide thirteen feet in one hour. From Coney Island to the Fire Island inlet, nine sailing vessels were destroyed, with a loss of twenty-one lives.

Fifteen years later, during another brutal winter, two shipwrecks took place. On November 20, 1836, the American ship *Bristol* went down off the Rockaways with 127 passengers on board, most of whom were Irish immigrants seeking a new life. On January 3, 1837, the American barque *Mexico* ran aground off the shore of Hempstead Beach (now Long Beach). In this disaster, 108 persons lost their lives. The dead from both these disasters were buried in what became known as Mariner's Lot. An obelisk monument was erected in the old Sand Hole Methodist Church cemetery, now called Rockville Cemetery, at Ocean Avenue and Merrick Road. The following is inscribed on the monument: "In this grave from the wide

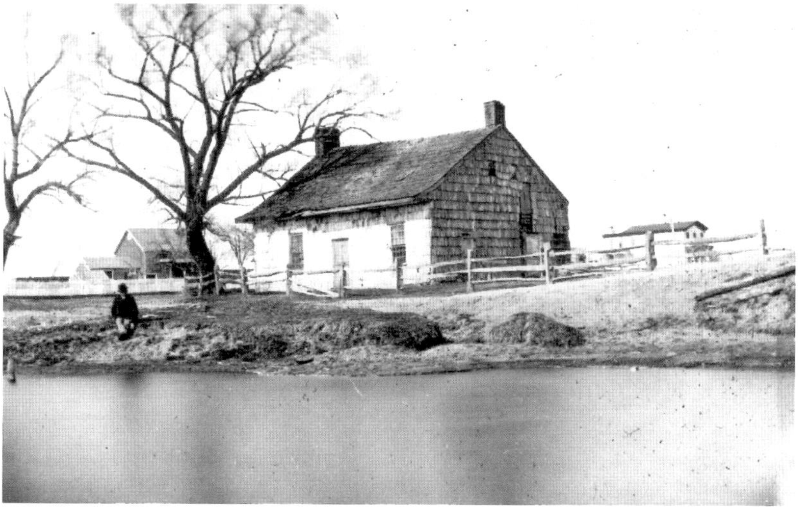

The Smith Farm and Pond, the birthplace of the Reverend Mordecai Rock Smith. *Courtesy of the Nassau County Photographic Archive.*

ocean doth sleep the bodies of those that crossed the deep. And instead of being landed safely on the shore on a cold frosty night they all were no more."

By 1839, Mordecai Rock Smith had become a preacher, as well as a miller, and was the pastor of the Sand Hole Methodist Church. In the early spring of that year, the deep snow on the Hempstead Plains began to melt, sending a torrent of water down the Mill River Valley. Smith reacted decisively and quickly by opening his mill's floodgates and emptying his pond, saving his milldam from the same fate as his fellow millers whose dams were destroyed.

The Reverend Smith would earn an even better distinction thanks to Robert Pettit, an entrepreneur and visionary who purchased a farm and homestead on Merrick Road near Lincoln Avenue in 1848. After opening a general store in his home, Pettit applied for permission from the United States government to open a post office in the store. Pettit and his neighbors thought it only fitting to name their settlement after the leading citizen of the day, the Reverend Mordecai Rock Smith, by then eighty-four years old. After trying Smithtown, Smithville and Rockville, Pettit was granted a post office under the name Rockville Centre, as it is still known today.

At the same time, the city of Brooklyn was facing a water shortage and sent its chief engineer, William McAlpine, to the area to measure the flow of water in Mill River and all the streams from Jamaica to Rockville Centre. The first purchase made by the Brooklyn Water Works Company was Leonard Cornell's millpond. The pond was enlarged and renamed Hempstead Pond. Seeking even more water, the company also purchased Smith's millpond. They planned to put in a pumping station and an aqueduct to carry water from Rockville Centre to Richmond Hill, where it would be pumped to a reservoir atop the hill for distribution to Brooklyn. By 1873, the Brooklyn Water Works had purchased all of the Mill River Valley, signaling the demise of the milling industry founded in 1710. The largest storage reservoir was built, creating Hempstead Lake.

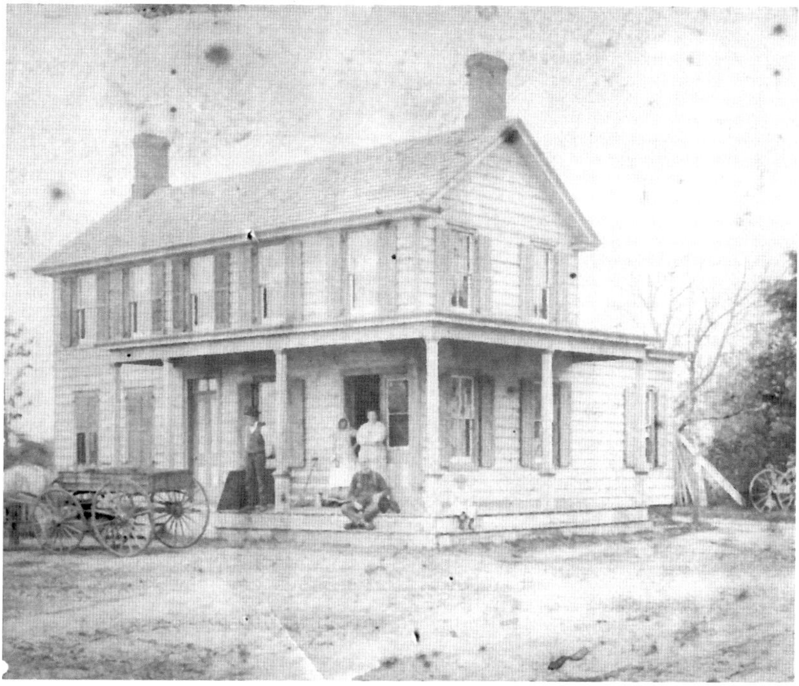

Robert Pettit's General Store, the site of Rockville Centre's first post office. Pettit, along with two partners, would build the first real estate development.

The project was moving along so quickly that a longtime resident of the area became disoriented. After wandering around for some time, he finally encountered someone to ask where he was and was heard to mutter, "Modern improvements were a humbug." It seems he was right, for soon a debate arose between McAlpine Associates and the Brooklyn Water Board over whether the project was really feasible. McAlpine lost the debate, and a contract was given to Kingsley and Keeney to continue work on this ambitious project.

After several more years of work and an expenditure of $1,400,000, the reservoir and several others that were built could never be completely filled due to the sandy bottoms of the ponds. While there were hard feelings among the people of Brooklyn, the citizens of Rockville Centre acquired a beautiful lake and migrating birds in an area that today is Hempstead Lake State Park.

Chapter 2

LOCATION, LOCATION, LOCATION

Robert Pettit, John P. Rhodes and Julius Auerbach purchased the Mordecai Rock Smith farm, subdividing it into residential lots with three roads running through it: Banks Avenue (nearest the pond), Centre Avenue and Village Avenue.

These three enterprising men ran an advertisement in several newspapers throughout Queens County. In the following advertisement, Pettit, Rhodes and Auerbach effectively employed the first rule of real estate—location, location, location: "The site is unsurpassed within the state for salubrity of climate, and beauty of location. It lies on a natural terrace commanding an extensive view of the country. Gentlemen wishing a country seat will find it to their advantage to secure lots in said village."

Among the new families moving to Rockville Centre was a group of sea captains, both retired and active, and their families, many of them from Maine. The first to arrive was Captain Edwin F. Wallace, who acquired a large tract of land along Maple Avenue. Captain Wallace went on to become

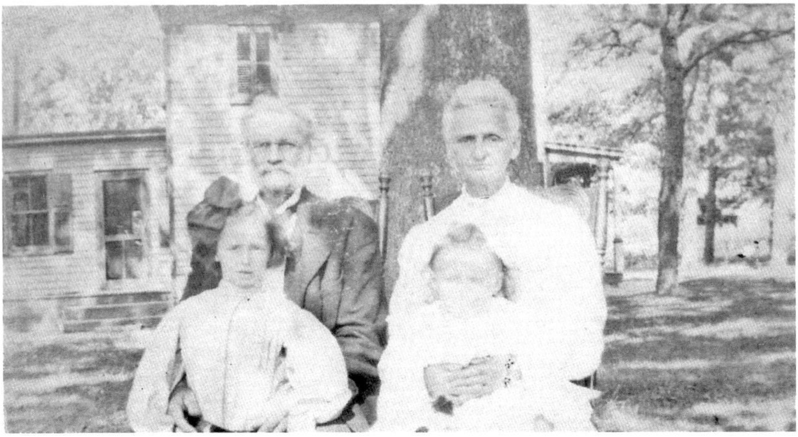

Captain John Driscoll, with wife Sara and granddaughters Elizabeth and Grace. This photograph was taken at their home on Rockaway Avenue.

instrumental in the incorporation of the village. The site of his home is now the Village Green.

Also living on Maple Avenue was Captain James W. Carty, who had his home in Harrington, Maine, broken down, shipped to Rockville Centre and rebuilt. Other sea captains scattered throughout the area were Captain John Driscoll and Joseph W. Proctor.

Driscoll captained five ships during his long career at sea, the first being the schooner *Davison* out of East Rockaway. He met his wife, Sara Johnson, through her father, Captain William Johnson, of Brooklyn. Married on December 23, 1862, they took up residence on Rockaway Avenue. Eventually, they became the parents of eleven children.

Captain Proctor lived on Clinton Avenue after moving from Buck's Harbor, Maine. After captaining both sailing ships and steamers, he served on the school board in the early 1900s.

The majority of the captains' homes were clustered along North Village Avenue in the area known as the Grove. A new road was cut through and named Maine Avenue in honor of these courageous seafarers. Captain Austin Jayne's home

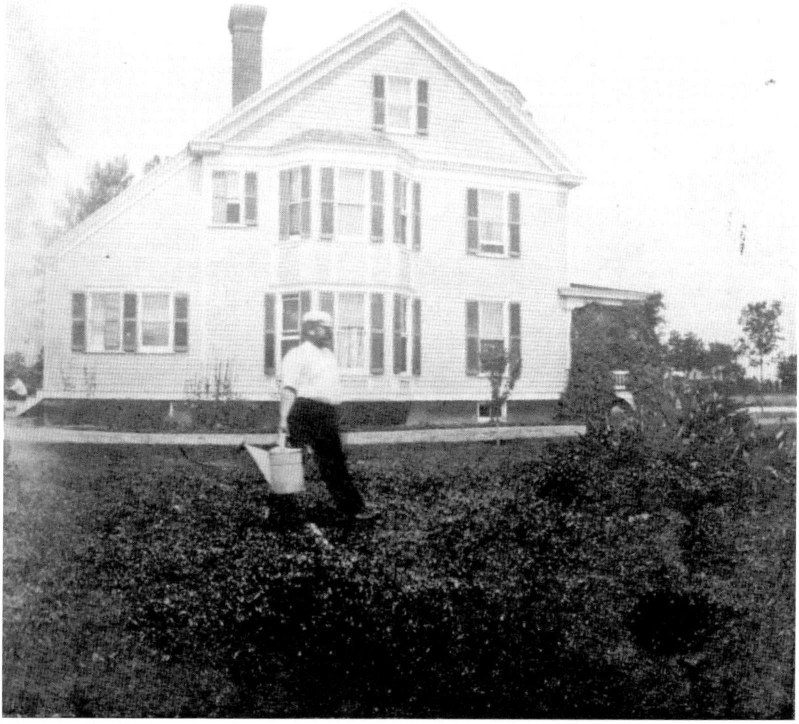

Captain Joseph W. Proctor, at his home on Clinton Avenue, hailed from Buck's Harbor, Maine. Proctor went on to become an early school board member.

was built on the crest of a slight rise, affectionately known as Barnacle Hill. Joining him in the Grove were Captains James Gallison, Samuel F. Phillips, Charles Coombes, Walter Whittmore and Tristram Thurlow Corbett. Captain Phillips's home was moved to 28 Hempstead Avenue during America's bicentennial celebration. It now serves as the Museum of the Village of Rockville Centre, where this narrative is being written.

Due to the rise in population and housing, many goods and services were required. Some of the early retail establishments carried dry goods, groceries, dress trimmings, millinery goods, boots and shoes. Other businesses carried wood, fuel,

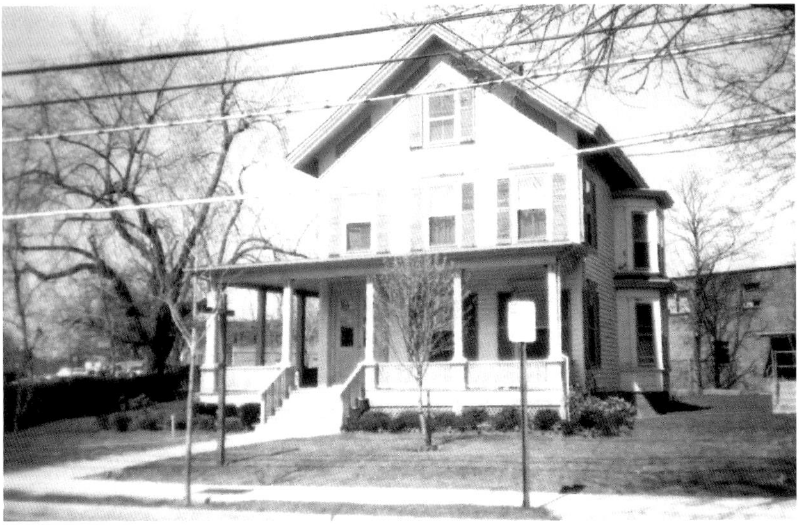

The Captain Samuel F. Phillips house after it was moved to Hempstead Avenue in 1975 to become the Museum of the Village of Rockville Centre.

fertilizer, sashes, blinds, doors and moldings. One of these latter establishments was the G.D. Combes Estate, founded in 1868 by Clinton F. Combes at the corner of Merrick Road and Centre Avenue. When his son, Glentworth D. Combes, took over after his father's death, the business was moved to Park Avenue and the railroad tracks. It was so close, in fact, that an engine pulling and delivering a car full of corn struck it. The office was pushed two feet or more into the street. The chimneys were knocked down, but strangely enough, the canned goods remained on the shelves. Fortunately, there were no injuries reported.

Another of these early shops was Thurston's Drug Store. Mr. and Mrs. Edward T. Thurston purchased all the land between Park and Village Avenues and Merrick Road and Cherry Street (now Lincoln Avenue). Their home and shop occupied one building on the corner of Merrick Road and Village Avenue. For thirty-eight years, "Doc" Thurston's remained a village landmark.

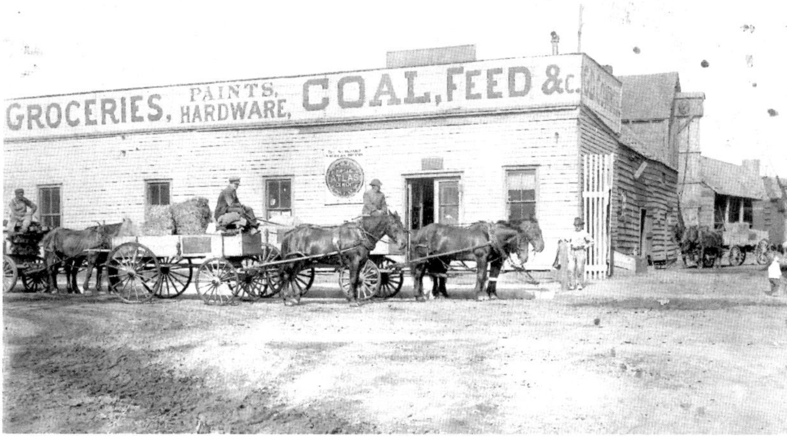

Above: The G.D. Combes estate, a hardware and lumber business, originally founded by Clinton F. Combes in 1868 on Merrick Road near Centre Avenue.

Below: Thurston's Drug Store and residence stood at the corner of Merrick Road and Village Avenue, where it remained a landmark for thirty-eight years.

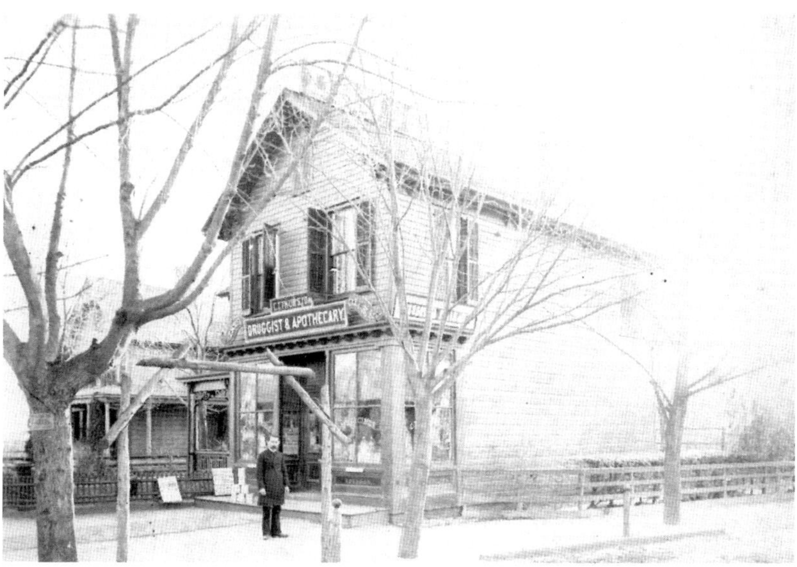

While most proprietors were men, one woman, Mrs. Mary A. Cock, ran a shop selling stoves, tinware and house furnishings. She would begin a trend of women's entrepreneurship that still grows today in Rockville Centre and beyond.

Although groceries, meats, produce and baked goods were often delivered in horse-drawn drays outfitted with drawers and shelves—a store on wheels, if you will—homemakers of the day also looked forward to Saturday evenings, when not only local residents but residents of neighboring villages came to the Centre to shop along Village Avenue. They also came to visit with one another, share the latest news, solve domestic problems, debate local issues and listen to the many hawkers offering such diverse wares as bunion cures, medical miracles, work shirts, cooking utensils and neckties. A fun time was had by all.

When the South Side Railroad steamed into the station in 1867, it carried on board many captains of industry and their families seeking a breath of fresh air and a break from city life. Along with the railroad came Rockville Centre's first newspaper, the *Picket*, published by John H. Reed. By the joining of these two forces, the community began declaring its independence from the town of Hempstead and the larger territory known as Near Rockaway.

Soon the *Picket*, a weekly newspaper, began running advertisements for hotels to accommodate summer visitors from Brooklyn and New York City. Rockville Centre was fast becoming a resort town due, in part, to its proximity to the sea and sand along the south shore of Long Island.

Back's Hotel opened on Woods Avenue and was owned and operated by Anna K. Back, a German immigrant. Many people from as far away as Woodhaven took the trolley to stop number 112 to enjoy the German cuisine and ambiance. For thirty-five years, the hotel was the scene of the Grand Annual Masquerade Ball. Admission was twenty-five cents, including hatcheck.

Back's Hotel was sold to Karl Wegener Sr. in 1929 and renamed the Arbor Inn Restaurant. It was named for the

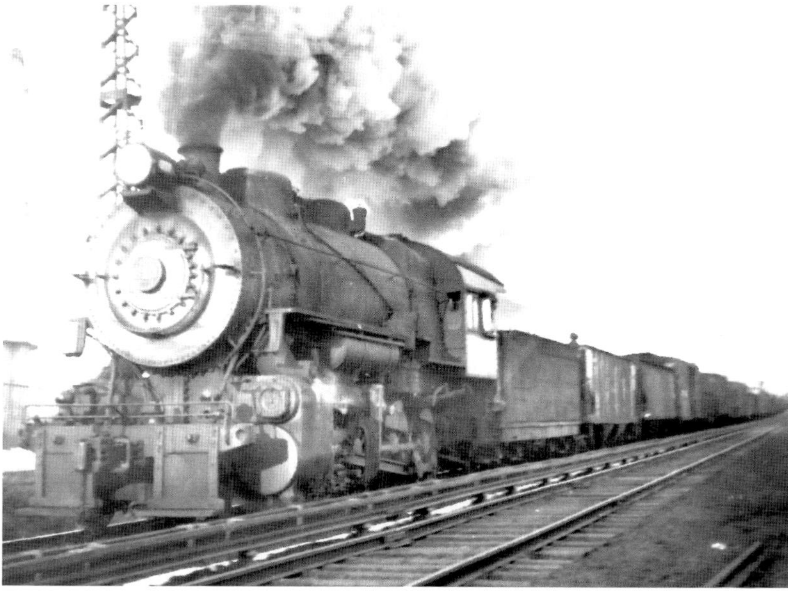

The South Side Railroad steamed into the station in 1867, bringing many new residents and summer visitors to Rockville Centre.

rather large grape arbor on the property. Wegener, himself a German, kept an eye on every detail, even creating his own flower arrangements. The restaurant served both German and continental cuisine. It was Rockville Centre's most popular dining spot for many years. It was certainly this author's favorite.

The Claremont Hotel played host to a wealthy upper-class clientele, among them Mrs. Andrew Carnegie. The hotel would pick up its guests at the station in polished carriages drawn by plume-decked horses. The Claremont would eventually become the Knickerbocker Hotel, owned by Treadwell Carpenter, businessman, banker and village trustee. Once again, it would change hands and become the Carlten House. It served the community for many years before being destroyed by fire. An office building now occupies the site at the corner of Merrick Road and Morris Avenue.

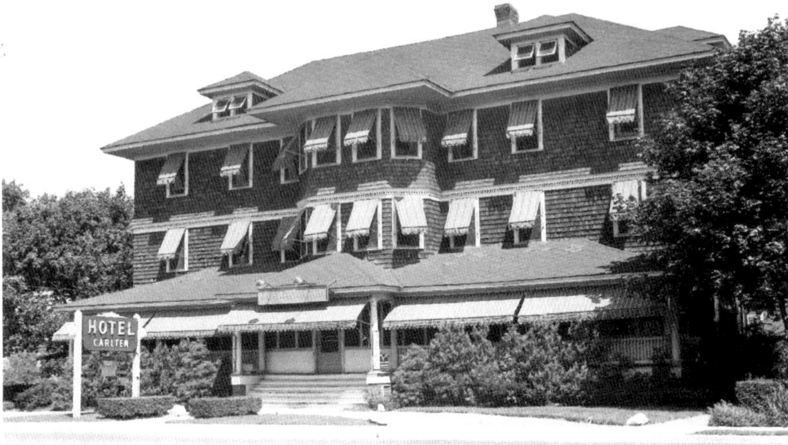

The Hotel Carlten was the third hotel to be located at the corner of Merrick Road and Morris Avenue. Its predecessors were the Knickerbocker and Claremont.

Henry Lotz owned and operated the Henry House, which burned down while he was in Europe. The year was 1888, famous for the great blizzard. In its place, the Lotz Hotel rose like a phoenix from the ashes. At three stories high, it was the tallest building in Rockville Centre. From its German clock tower, on a clear day, one could see all the way to Long Beach. The hotel's grand opening took place in 1889, with two hundred people in attendance.

The Brick Hotel, as it was called by the locals, became a commercial traveler's paradise, complete with a bar, dining room, bowling alley and lodge rooms. The hotel had its own power plant supplying electricity and a water tank on its upper floor. On the first floor were the main desk, lounge and barbershop. On the third floor, the Odd Fellows' members met and dances were held. For many years, the hotel played host to the village court, located on the second floor.

Rockville Centre had a mini industrial revolution of sorts when several factories became part of the landscape. Anton

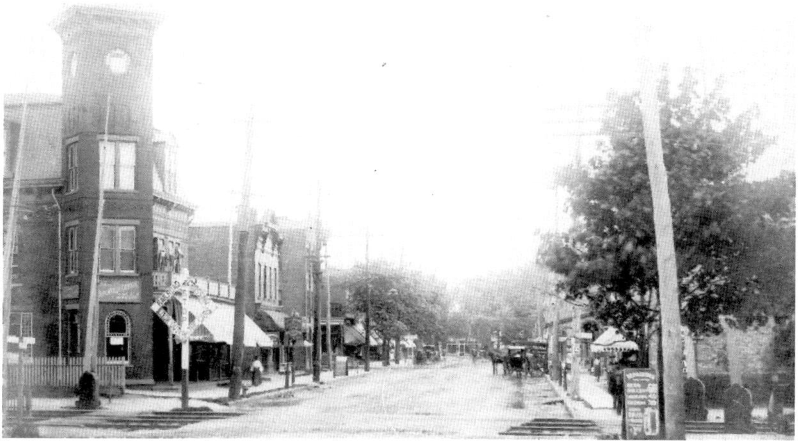

The Lotz "Brick" Hotel stood on the east side of North Village Avenue and became a commercial travelers' paradise. *Courtesy of Charles and Nellie Huttunen.*

Kessler's large tailoring business was on the site where St. Agnes's convent now serves as a community outreach center and bishop's residence. During the Civil War, the Kesslers made thousands of uniforms for the Union army. Women drove to Hicksville to pick up the materials needed to make the uniforms in their own homes.

Charles Losea operated a blacksmith and wheelwright business in the rear of his home on the north side of Merrick Road, just west of Village Avenue. He built farm wagons, drays, carriages and the first fire apparatus. After the parts were produced, they went to the second floor for painting and then were sent back downstairs for assembly. It was said that "he did work of the best quality."

A.V.S. Hicks's Hammock Company's first product was called the Centennial Hammock, which came in smaller sizes for babies and was more convenient than a cradle. He later produced fishnets, fly nets for horses and net school bags for children.

The Kayser Glove Company opened a factory on North Park Avenue between Front Street and College Place. An early advertisement read: "Girls wanted for permanent positions, to learn the glove business; good chance for advancement to steady workers; pay while learning."

As the era drew to a close, the *Picket* was sold to George Wallace, and the name changed to the *South Side Observer*. Wallace championed such causes as schools and banking, also calling for incorporation and the formation of Nassau County.

Chapter 3

VILLAGE VICISSITUDE

Rockville Centre's residential renaissance was in full swing. A bustling business district was booming, houses of worship were springing up toward the heavens, schools and a library were being established for higher learning and a lyceum circuit lecture hall and theater was bringing culture and entertainment to the residents.

George Wallace of the *South Side Observer* was described as an erstwhile schoolteacher, lawyer and someone who cherished some political ambition. His brother Charles L. Wallace was a popular real estate broker. They shared the duties of both publisher and editor.

The *Observer* had a fairly aggressive editorial policy. In its first year, several editorials ran calling for better schools, a bank, village incorporation and a new county government. One of these editorials stated: "A new schoolhouse of tasteful architecture and capable of accommodating a large number of children with the appropriate number of teachers, is now almost a necessity. Good schoolhouses and churches add very much to the appearance and enhance the value of any village, and we believe from the movement now being made, the enterprising people of Rockville Centre will not be behind much longer in this respect." Liturgies, lessons and literature, oh my!

When the Methodist congregation split from the old Sand Hole Church, it erected a rather rustic structure called the Tabernacle on Banks Avenue near Merrick Road. Later, St. Mark's Methodist Church purchased land from Robert Pettit on the southwest corner of Village Avenue and Merrick Road. A church was erected with a tall, symmetrical steeple, and a cornerstone was laid. The first pastor was the Reverend W.J. Robinson. The church stood at this location for many years before being destroyed by fire. St. Mark's Methodist Church now stands on Hempstead Avenue.

Simultaneously, or so it seemed, a Baptist congregation held its earliest services in the Rockville Centre Railroad Station, where it also held Sunday school classes. The First Baptist Church was built in the late Victorian style of architecture, with many stained-glass windows. The interior sat 175 worshipers, and the walls and ceiling were magnificently wainscoted by master carpenter and craftsman William T. Odell. The building still stands across from the current post office on Merrick Road and now plays host to the Vineyard Church.

As the population continued to grow, people of other denominations also moved their families to Rockville Centre. Two of these new residents, Sylvester Gildersleeve and Francis F. Wilson, set to work establishing Episcopal services. They were able to secure Institute Hall, as it was suitably located and was already furnished with seats and an organ. So it was under the authorization of Episcopal bishop Littlejohn that an Episcopal mission was formed in Rockville Centre. Soon after, a church was erected at the corner of Village Avenue and Quealy Place, and services commenced. The first resident minister was the Reverend Charles Martin Niles. During his stay he acted as lay reader, deacon and priest in charge. Today, the congregation still worships in the original church building.

In a small white church with a tall steeple, a group of Lutherans held a meeting for the purpose of incorporating

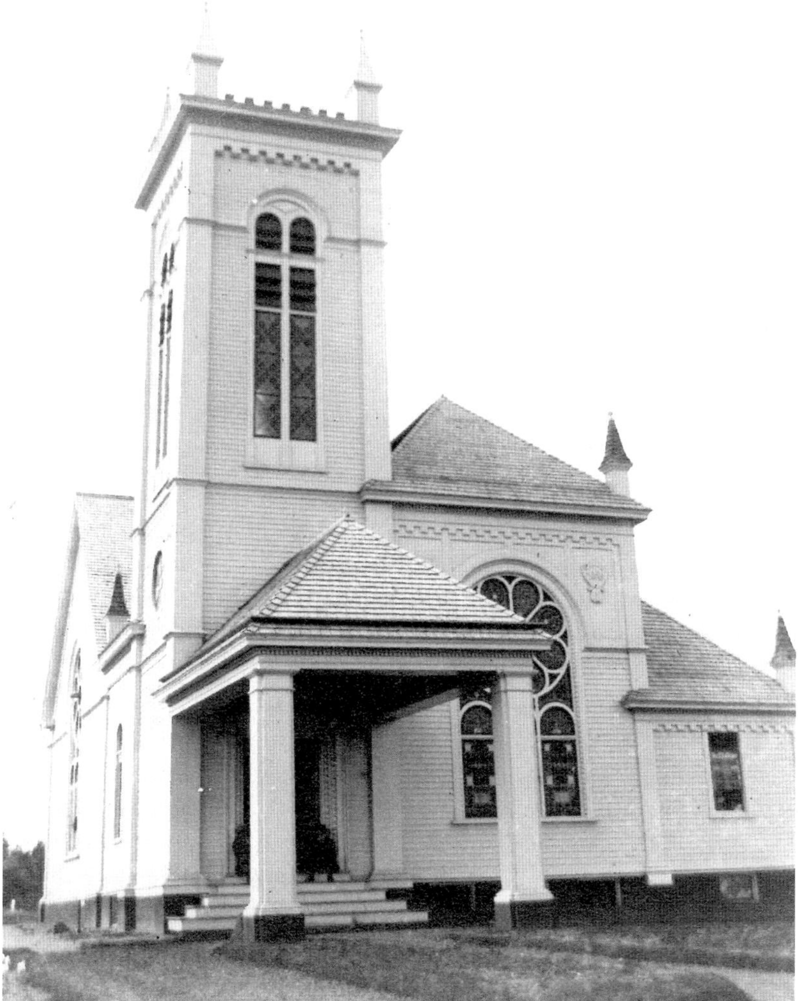

St. Mark's Methodist Church when it was located at the corner of Village Avenue and Merrick Road. It was eventually destroyed by fire.

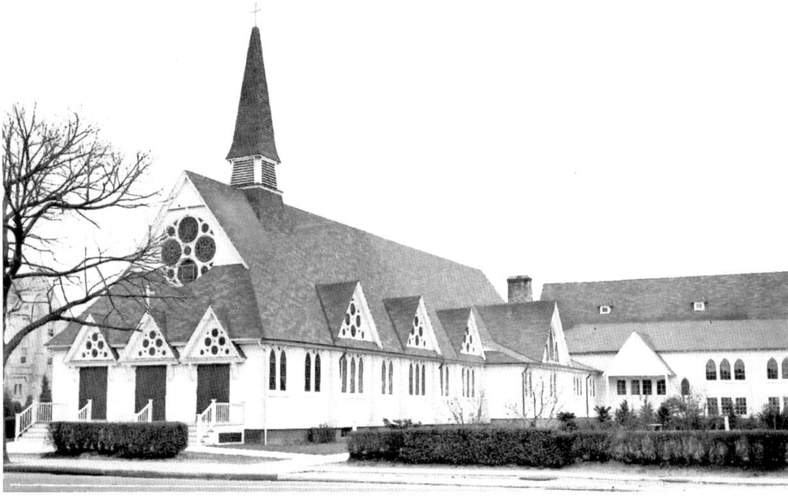

The Ascension Episcopal Church held its first service on March 29, 1891. Today's congregation still worships in the original building on North Village Avenue.

a congregation, adopting a constitution and electing officers. Among this group was Reverend C. Armand Miller, pastor of the Holy Trinity Lutheran Church in New York City. It was in his honor that this new congregation named its church, the English Evangelical Lutheran Church of the Holy Trinity. The church, which now stands at Lincoln and Woodland Avenues, has grown into one of the largest congregations in the village.

When the first attempt at establishing a school district was thwarted, the people of Rockville Centre were determined to have a school of their own and decided to build an institute and have in it one or more competent teachers. The Rockville Centre Institute, also known as Burr's Private School, was organized in October 1871, and a cornerstone was laid in November of the same year. Located on the corner of Hempstead and Village Avenues, the institute opened on June 3, 1872, with all the modern appliances of the day. Its curriculum prepared pupils either for business or college.

The first principal was W.C. Scovil; however, by the following September, he was succeeded by J.W. Cheney.

Soon, Rockville Centre School District 21 was established, and the first Board of Education was composed of Robert White, Robert Rea and John R. Sprague. This newly formed school district had a budget of $390, which consisted of $300 for teachers' salaries and $90 for classroom rentals. The first classes were held in Noble A. Taylor's house on Washington Street, a house on Merrick Road owned by John Storp and the Methodist Tabernacle on Banks Avenue.

These first public school classrooms, in rented quarters, were devoid of any school furniture, blackboards or textbooks. They could in no way compete with the newly opened institute. All of this began to change when a new, commodious, fully equipped public schoolhouse was built on College Place. The structure was twenty-eight by fifty feet and was two stories high, surmounted by a cupola and painted white with green shutters. There were three entrances, one in front for teachers and visitors, one on the east for boys and one on the west for girls. Rockville Centre now had school facilities unequaled by any of its sister villages.

Between the institute and the new public school lay Wright's Pond. The pond was popular with skaters in winter. When snow coated the ice, it was cleaned off by the boys. They could skate north over the pond almost to DeMott Avenue and south to Centre Avenue, in some places through alder bushes.

As time went on, the institute lost its prestige and eventually ceased to function as an educational institution. It was divided up and moved to the southeast corner of Village Avenue and Observer Street, now Sunrise Highway. There were two or three stores in the building at street level. Unfortunately, Wright's Pond was filled in and became, in part, the parking lot behind what was Clinton Avenue School and is now St. Agnes School. So, as that old song goes, "they paved paradise and put up a parking lot."

As the population was still increasing, so did the Board of Education and school enrollment. The board was now

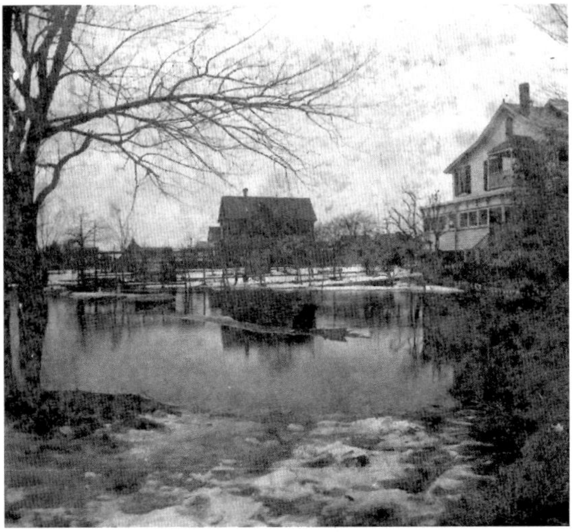

Wright's Pond once stood at the corner of Hempstead and Village Avenues. Eventually, it was filled in to become a parking lot.

composed of five members: Eden Sprout, Robert A. Davison, F.T. Johnson, William H. Jones and Francis F. Wilson. School enrollment increased from fifty-four pupils to seventy, and the school budget rose to $2,737.74. Wilson, who had been principal of a private school in New York City and then president of the school board, was keenly interested in maintaining a high academic standard in the local schools. He began taking steps to have Rockville Centre's schools recognized by the State Board of Regents.

As there was no public school on the south side of Long Island, outside of Greater New York, that offered high school work, Frank W. Lindley, a school principal, joined Wilson in envisioning a new academic department serving a large area along the south shore.

A citizens' visiting committee was appointed to visit the schools at least once a month and report back to the Board of Education on the conditions there. The committee consisted of the following members: Dr. F.M. Hexamer, Reverend L.D. Sammis, G.S. Roberts, Laura W. Warriner and Eliza E. Hutcheson. It should be noted that women were beginning to vote in school board elections some thirty years before the passage of the Nineteenth Amendment.

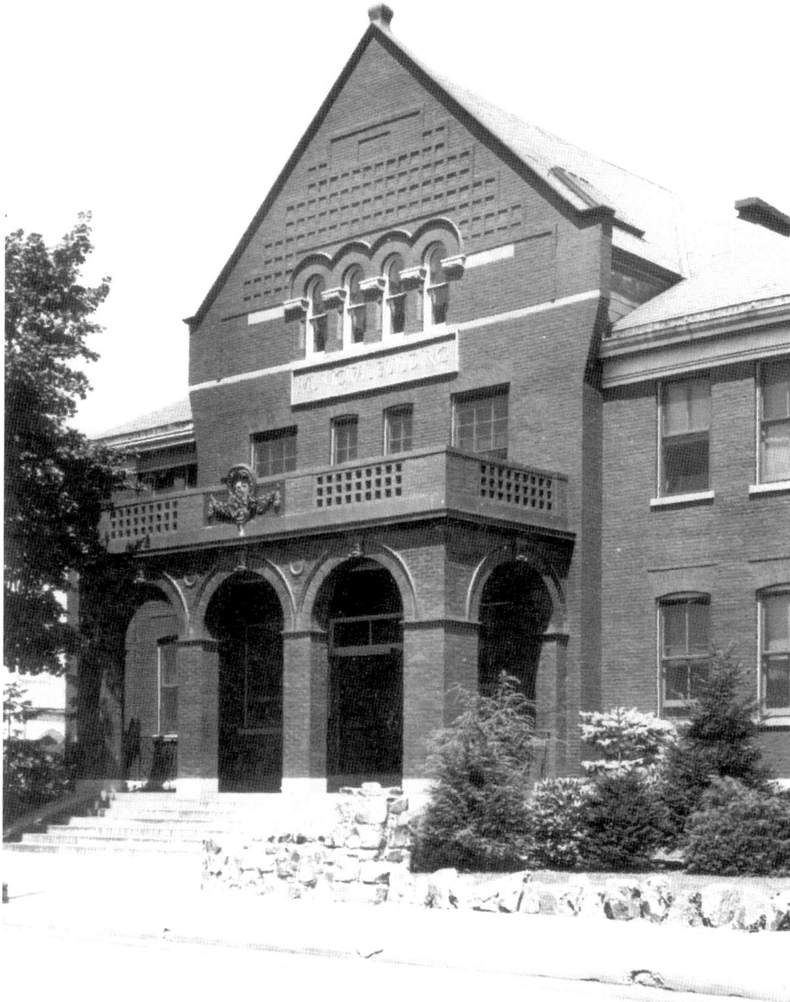

South Side High School, the first of its kind east of Jamaica, opened on February 20, 1892. It welcomed both resident and nonresident students.

It was found and reported that the current schoolhouse had become badly overcrowded, so on July 17, 1890, a petition was signed by fifty citizens of Rockville Centre and sent to the Board of Education. In compliance with this petition, a special school district meeting was held for the purpose of voting for or against the erection of a high school building. The vote was forty-three to twenty-four in favor.

South Side High School opened on February 20, 1892, with an enrollment of 281 resident pupils and 35 nonresident pupils. The school building now houses the Eugene J. Murray Village Hall.

In his annual address to the school district on August 3, 1892, Wilson announced the hiring of Elmer S. Redmond as principal of the new high school. In closing his address, Wilson said, "And we publish to the world at large that whoever wishes to have his children properly educated and prepared for college free of all costs, should hire, buy or build a house in Rockville Centre." This very sentiment still holds true today.

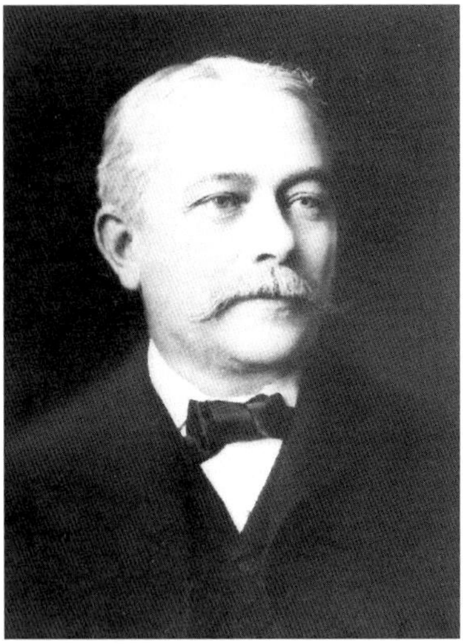

Francis French Wilson was active in Rockville Centre's schools, library, bank and the Ascension Episcopal Church. *Courtesy of Rockville Centre Public Library.*

With the opening of the new high school, a proposal was made from the Board of Education to the Rockville Centre Library and Improvement Association, founded in 1882 and housed on the second floor of the DeMott Building. The proposal was twofold: one, for the combining of the school's and association's book collections; and two, that the association become a library under the New York State Regents. The proposal was accepted, and the Free Public Library was formed. A board of trustees was composed of Francis F. Wilson, Robert A. Davison and Dr. Devillo N. Bulson from the school board, with Dr. Frank T. DeLano and Samuel F. Phillips from the association.

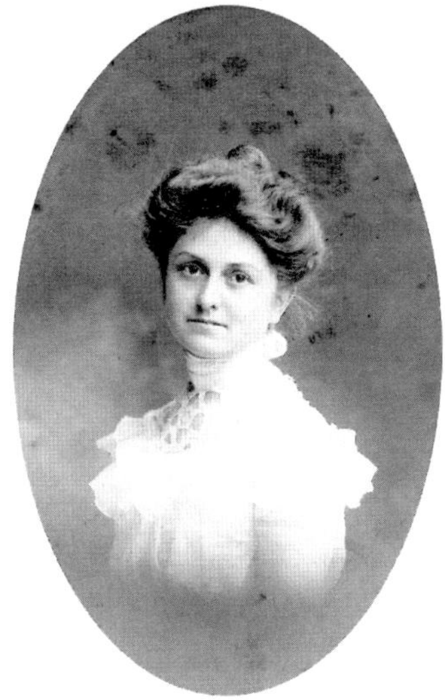

Sarah S. Field, the first paid librarian, used her talent as a singer to raise funds for purchasing books. *Courtesy of Rockville Centre Public Library.*

A provisional charter was granted by the regents, and Elmer S. Redmond, principal of the high school, was asked to also serve as supervising librarian. He was assisted by two students, Grace W. Dana and Sarah S. Field, who would succeed Redmond by becoming the first paid librarian. As Rockville Centre had no paved streets or sidewalks and was illuminated only by oil lanterns placed in front of homeowners' properties, Field often had to wear boots to work. On winter evenings, she carried a lantern to light her way home. Field's duties did not end when she left the library each day; her talent as a singer was put to good use at the socials held by the school and library to raise money to purchase books.

When the Library Association was housed in the DeMott Building, a clubroom was in use as the center of the village's social life, as well as a place to hold dances. In addition, Atheneum Hall, owned and operated by a woman, opened in a three-story building on the northwest corner of Village Avenue and Observer Street. At the ground level were the stores of grocers, butchers and fruiterers. The basement housed bowling alleys, which were open every evening except Sundays.

On June 27, 1888, the hall held its grand opening. The entertainment for the evening included the Meigs Sisters

Quartet and Alfred E. Pearsall, an elocutionist/humorist. The ticket price was seventy-five cents, and the opening night audience was made up of residents from Rockville Centre, Baldwin, Pearsall's Corners (now Lynbrook), Freeport, East Rockaway and Oceanville (now Oceanside).

In 1889, Marshall P. Wilder, the most distinguished and highest-paid entertainer to ever perform at Atheneum Hall, appeared under the auspices of the Rockville Centre Odd Fellows Lodge. Wilder was much in demand as a humorist and edited several volumes of the *Anthology of American Humor*, which enjoyed excellent distribution. The second and third floors of the hall were used for such entertainments as church fairs, cakewalks, medicine shows, exhibitions by hypnotists and periodical productions of *Uncle Tom's Cabin*. Lyceum circuit lecturers brought their controversial viewpoints to the village, prompting lively discussions and debates.

The fire companies also held their annual balls at the hall. The dance portion of the program was held on the second floor until midnight, when the merrymakers moved the festivities to the third floor, where a sumptuous repast was served. Afterward, the dancing continued on the floor below and went on until the wee hours of the morning, when the dancers departed to the strains of "Home Sweet Home."

With the prospect of incorporation looming, the people of Rockville Centre once again proved their prowess as visionary pioneers of progress. They realized that purchasing power would aid in the growth of the community and that, combining the idle funds of residents with the fluid finances of businessmen and -women, they could create a larger fund capable of helping all.

Banking was definitely needed closer to home, as it took the better part of a day's journey to get to the banks already established in Hempstead, Far Rockaway and Jamaica. The Bank of Rockville Centre Trust Company was founded, chartered by the New York State authorities and opened for business on January 2, 1891, in the rear of John W. DeMott's

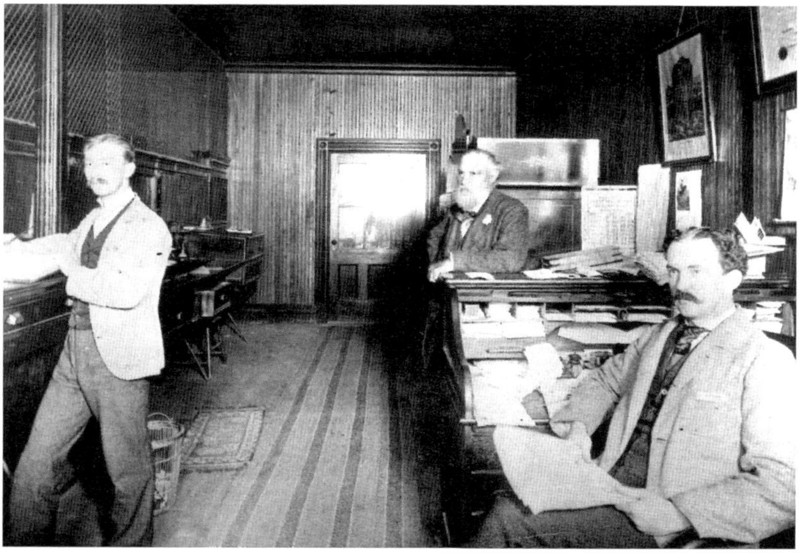

The Bank of Rockville Centre, circa 1891. Pictured (left to right) are Bergen T. Raynor, clerk; Charles W. Hayes, director; and Hiram R. Smith, president.

insurance agency. It not only served as a local bank, but it also served the surrounding communities of Baldwin, Lynbrook and East Rockaway. The first day's business resulted in deposits totaling $4,036.62.

In the early part of 1893, growth was slow but steady, and the young bank was looking forward to owning its own building. However, its optimistic and entirely proper preparations for expansion were defeated by one of those periodic depressions in business. Deposits were dropping, and the market value of certain securities declined rapidly. The bank was in danger of being closed.

After much discussion by the board of directors, Captain Samuel F. Phillips led the group to his opinion that to close the bank would not only involve loss of their capital but also their very reputations and self-respect. His plan was for the directors to make good the difference between market and book value of the securities. The sixteen men raised a fund of $20,500, which placed the bank once more in sound condition.

For many years, the *South Side Observer* ran editorials calling for the incorporation of the village. It took twenty-three years for the residents of Rockville Centre to see the merit of such an action. Atheneum Hall would become a polling place for votes to be cast in the most important issue of the day: incorporation.

The whole village was taking part in the discussions and debates, and excitement was rising. Did the populace want to finally declare their independence from the town of Hempstead and Queens County, only to bear the new taxes that surely would be levied? Or did they wish to eschew change and continue the status quo?

There were pros and cons aplenty, with one of the pros being the possibility of electricity, running water, indoor plumbing and telephone service. One of the cons was the loss of farmland and the doubling of the population. There was even a rumor that the twenty-six men who signed the election petition/notice were scheming to make themselves rich while they levied all kinds of taxes on the rest of the residents.

On the morning of July 15, 1893, the voting began at 10:00 a.m. at Atheneum Hall and continued until 3:00 p.m. Voting was going slowly until the resident commuters returned home for the day at 2:30 p.m., a half hour before the polls closed. The results of the election were posted in the *South Side Observer*. There were 219 votes polled, of which 139 were in favor of incorporation, 79 against and 1 blank, making a majority of 60 in favor of incorporation.

A new era was dawning, and Rockville Centre was now under home rule. The first village election was held on August 19, 1893, again at Atheneum Hall, and the following men were elected to office: president, John Lyon; trustees, Captain Edwin Wallace, Edwin D. Seabury and Glentworth D. Combes; treasurer, Nelson L. Seaman; and tax collector, Charles A. Spedick.

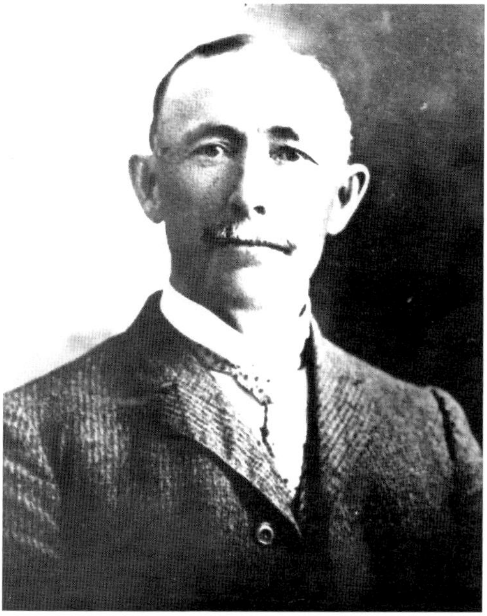

Attorney John Lyon was elected Rockville Centre's first village president on July 15, 1893. *Courtesy of Rockville Centre Public Library.*

On August 26, 1893, the first village board meeting took place at the Maple Avenue home of Trustee Wallace. At the meeting, the new village board took on the many concerns of a growing suburban community, such as safety issues, water supply, electricity and telephone communication. They also worked out a village budget; it was going to cost $1,300 annually to run the village. The general tax levy would be thirteen cents per $100 of assessed valuation, and later there would be an additional tax levy of twenty-two cents per $100 for highway improvements.

Several ordinances were adopted. A speed limit was set at eight miles per hour to stop young hooligans from racing through the streets in clouds of dust. One anecdote has it that Mae Irene Hamel and Dr. Devillo N. Bulson also raced their buggies around the village whenever they met on the roads. They probably were not the only adults having a bit of fun. The fine for these infractions was fixed at five dollars. Hamel, a summer resident, eventually married Francis F. Wilson Jr., a local architect. The other ordinances included requiring

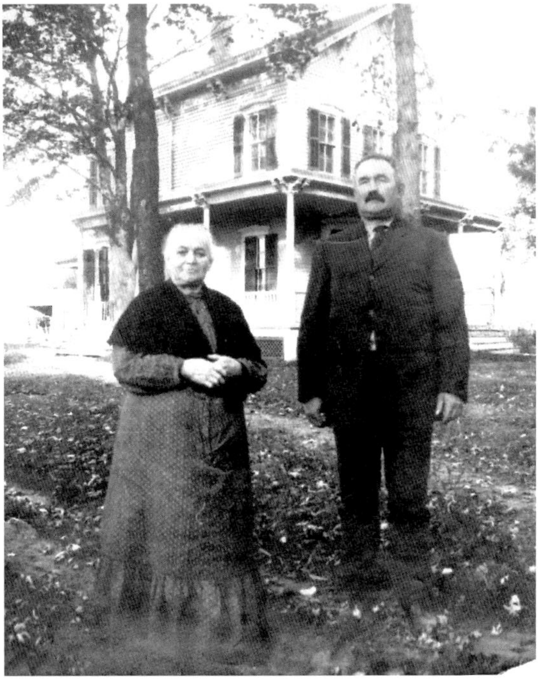

Captain and Mrs. Edwin F. Wallace in front of their home on Maple Avenue, site of the first village board meeting, now the Village Green.

peddlers to obtain licenses and that all dogs running at large be muzzled.

In the area of safety, the Eureka Hook, Ladder and Bucket Company was formed. The buckets were made by local tinsmith J.F. Fox, and the first fire truck was built by Charles H. Losea and delivered for the sum of $150. Not long after the truck was delivered, Foreman John R. Sprague had the men outfitted in uniforms. As it was shortly after the Civil War, he obtained flat peaked fatigue caps, black belts with red banding, red (later blue) shirts and dark trousers. These were probably made by local tailor Anton Kessler, who had made uniforms for the Union army. Drills were commenced at every full moon.

Shortly thereafter, the Live Oak Engine Company was established. It was named in honor of the famous volunteer company in New York City. A piece of property was purchased from Sarah E. Whitney, and the Live Oak

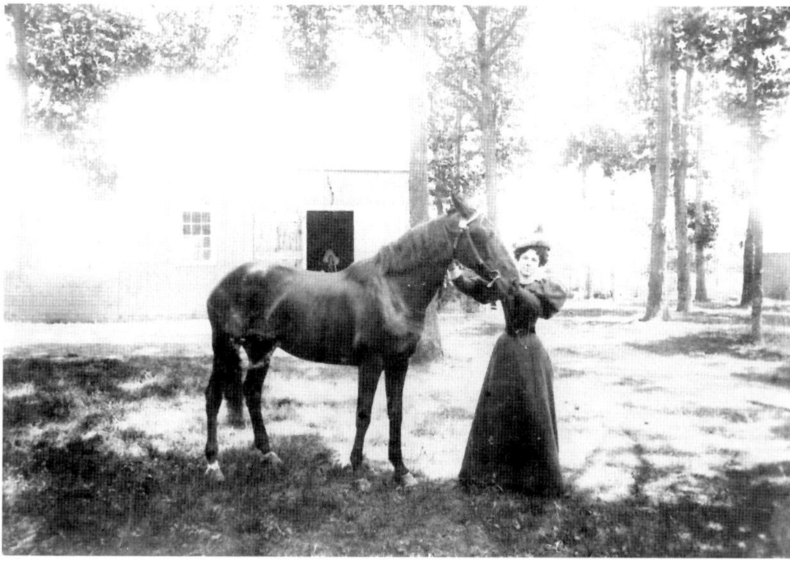

Summer resident Mae Irene Hamel and Dr. Devillo N. Bulson raced their horses around the village whenever they met on the roads.

firefighters immediately began building their firehouse. After taking possession of their new fire engine, a parade of the Eureka and Live Oak Companies took place. They paraded through the village, and a "wash" was held to test the engine at William Whitney's pond at Centre Avenue and Willoughby Street.

For several years, at the sound of the fire whistle, a gallant group of women did everything from helping to pull the fire engine to pulling the frozen boots from the firemen's feet. They also made coffee and carried it to the members fighting the fires. This unofficial women's auxiliary helped pay off the mortgage on the firehouse by holding several large fairs.

By 1875, the Eureka and Live Oak fire companies were joined by the Alert and Defender Hose Companies. After organizing the Rockville Centre Fire Department, a budget of $2,000 was put in place by the village. It soon became apparent that the newly formed department was hampered by

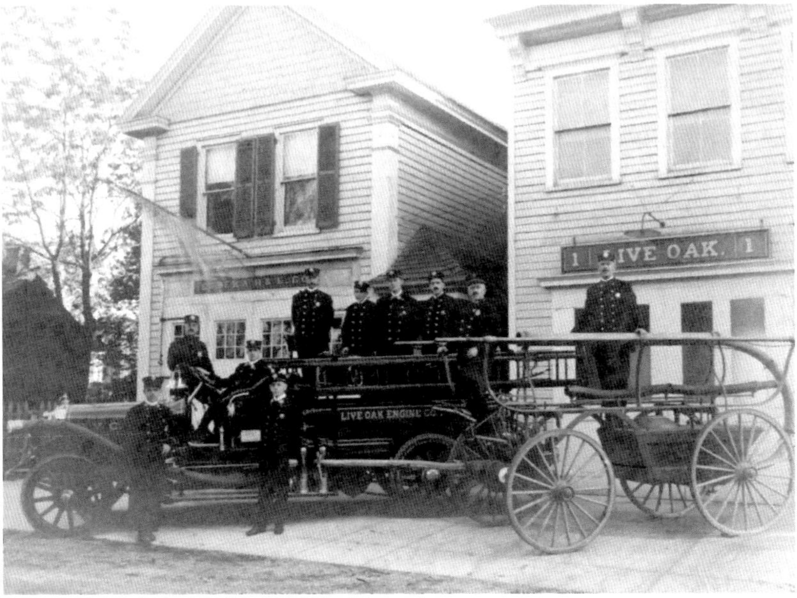

Rockville Centre's first two firehouses, belonging to Eureka Hook, Ladder and Bucket Company and the Live Oak Engine Company on Washington Street.

the lack of an adequate water supply. Property was purchased by the village at the corner of Maple and Morris Avenues. A small pump house was built and a steam pump installed. The water came from a shallow well on the property, and soon thereafter, two more shallow wells were dug. Water mains were laid, first in the business district and then in the residential areas, providing running water to all.

When an excess of steam from the pump house resulted, the village fathers decided to put it to work to provide electricity. Daniel D. Smith, uncle of Arthur DeMott, the future village treasurer and acting village clerk, was called in to set up Rockville Centre's electric system. By 1898, only fifteen years after the first electric generating plant in the United States opened in New York City, Rockville Centre had its own municipal power plant in operation. At the beginning, electricity was produced for lighting village streets, and the plant only operated at night. Gradually, homes and businesses came on line, and at one point, Rockville Centre's power plant supplied electric current to other nearby areas. This was, of course, prior to the laying of the Long Island Lighting Company's cables.

At the same time, another big concern was being addressed: that of street and highway improvements. For years, the byways were macadamized (oiled) to keep dust down in summer and during other dry spells that might occur. On June 7, 1898, the Village Board authorized a committee to study the possibility of purchasing a street sprinkling system. The system was either purchased or contracted out, and regular sprinkling commenced on Village Avenue from Lincoln Avenue to Washington Avenue. Front Street was also being sprinkled along the railroad tracks and Observer Street. The system proved so successful that the Long Island Rail Road sought and received permission to tap into the water main near the tracks at Village Avenue so it could sprinkle its roadbed, eliminating the dust kicked up by fast-moving trains.

Another innovation and improvement was about to make life even easier for Rockville Centre's residents and businesses: the telephone. The South Shore Telephone Company and the New York and New Jersey Telephone Company were both seeking permission from the village to erect poles and run lines. Permission was granted, with the understanding that the village office would receive a free phone and that both companies would make provisions to link their services to other companies' lines.

After being dubbed a "pretty village and a growing community attracting outsiders as a place of residence" by the *Brooklyn Daily Eagle*, Rockville Centre's population, once again, was growing. Almost every residence was surrounded by a fence and had a flagpole in its yard from which to fly "Old Glory." Buntings were added to welcome the members of the local chapter of the Grand Army of the Republic, a post–Civil War veterans' group. On Memorial Day throughout the 1880s and '90s, these Union army veterans would form a parade at the corner of Hempstead and Village Avenues. The parade then marched, to the beat of drums, to the Sand Hole Methodist Church Cemetery to decorate the graves of the men who had made the ultimate sacrifice.

The police department got its start when Constable Joseph A. Shelly was appointed and a local lockup was built. Two police justices—William H. Connell, once the president of the Library and Improvement Association, and John Vincent—were hired.

While the men of Rockville Centre were busy building the infrastructure and physical plants, the women were busying themselves through work on various committees and in organizations promoting the social and cultural activities in the village, creating not only a great place to live but a wonderful way of life as well. One of these organizations was (and still is) the Fortnightly Club of Rockville Centre, founded by Mary Haight in 1898. Seeking the guidance of Mrs. Adah Sawyer Gould Skilton, a member of several clubs in Brooklyn, Haight described the need for women to stay mentally alert, keep abreast of things going on in the world and cultivate an active interest in things and people beyond the limits of Rockville Centre. Or, as this author's mother used to say, "to use your head for more than a hat rack."

And so it was, on March 4, 1898, that a group of women was invited to Mary Haight's home to consider the advisability of organizing a club whose purpose was educational. Her idea for meeting every two weeks in each other's homes for the purpose of studying, more carefully, the principle issues of the day met with great favor. On April 2, 1898, a group of ten women attended the first meeting of the Fortnightly Club of Rockville Centre. This being the era of the Spanish-American War, the program of the day was Cuba and its prospects between the United States and Spain. After the program, the officers of the club were elected as follows: president, Adah Skilton; vice-president,

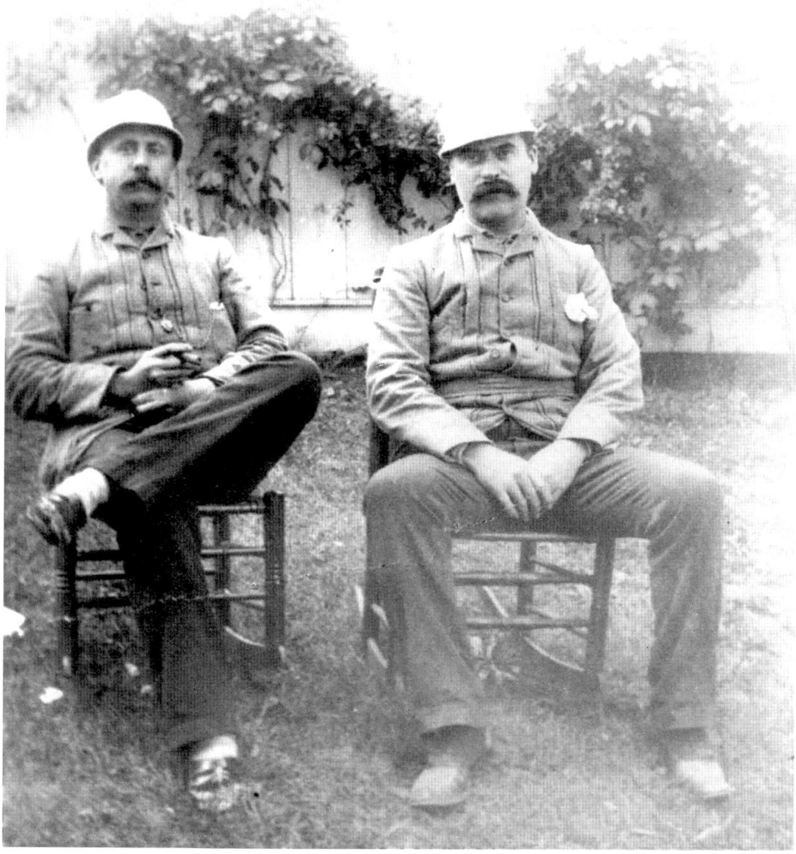

John Vincent and William H. Connell were hired as police justices when a police lockup was built on Maple Avenue.

Mary Haight; and secretary/treasurer, S. Albertson Glover. The women also decided to discuss new books and promote the study of drama, history and music.

The response to this new club was immediate, and it was not long before membership began to grow, so much so that membership had to be limited to thirty. Eventually, the

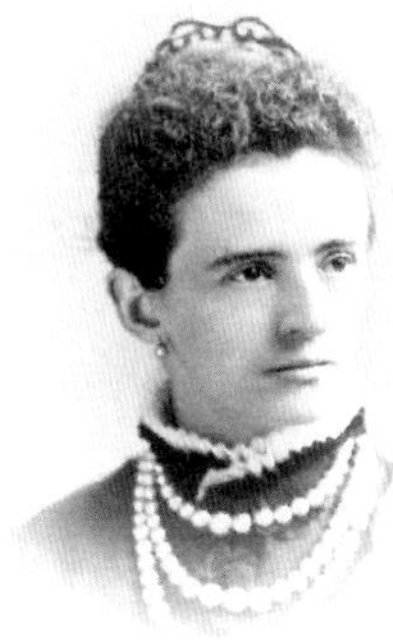

Adah Skilton, first president of the Fortnightly Club, was presented with a medal of merit by the New York Federation of Woman's Clubs.

membership rose to four hundred, and the club began to meet at Atheneum Hall and, later, the Ascension Church Hall and the Masonic Temple. Today, the club meets at St. Mark's Methodist Church on Hempstead Avenue and is still growing strong, nourishing women's minds, hearts and souls through camaraderie, creativity and community.

As a member of the Ascension Episcopal Church, Mary Haight persuaded then Reverend William E. Nies to create a special Easter edition of the local newspaper, which was contributed to, edited and managed by the women of the congregation. Haight convinced Nies it would be a lucrative venture, and he agreed. At a meeting of the Church Guild, the women decided to meet with George Wallace, publisher of the *South Side Observer*, at his office. Wallace agreed to let the women use his publication for a supplement to its Easter edition. However, the newspaper would only pay for the printing. He also specified that all funds acquired by the women from advertising were to go to the parish. The women were also to secure the material for the paper, contributed by writers, principally women.

Originally relying on the men to secure advertisements, it became clear that the women would have to do it themselves. They took several arduous journeys into New York City to visit the leading merchants of the day, raising the funds needed. Surprisingly easy, the women also secured all of the writers necessary for the special supplement. The Art Department of the high school held a contest for the best cover design, and the winner was a huge bunch of Easter lilies on a purple background. When the paper was finally issued on the Saturday before Easter, it was sold on the Long Island Rail Road trains and at all the newsstands on the South Shore. It was a great success.

As the nineteenth century drew to a close, the pioneering, progressive men and women of Rockville Centre were eagerly awaiting the beginning of the twentieth century and the continued growth it certainly would bring.

Chapter 4

CANTERBURY AND OTHER TALES

Rockville Centre at the turn of the twentieth century was experiencing unprecedented growth. The Long Island Rail Road's new Montauk division was bringing families to the country to live and making it easier for the captains of industry to commute to their businesses in Brooklyn and New York City. To accommodate these new families, homes were being built with lightning and, for Rockville Centre's well-established families, often frightening speed. Real estate developers were buying up farmland, cutting through roads and laying foundations all across the village.

One of the first female developers on Long Island lived right here in Rockville Centre. Anna Millar caused uneasiness among her male counterparts when she purchased land that they deemed worthless along Hempstead Avenue. Millar would prove them wrong by filling and grading the area, building and selling several homes at prices ranging from $5,000 to $7,000. All were of superior design and construction, containing hot water, heat, hardwood floors, tile baths and every convenience for both beauty and comfort.

Millar also developed sixteen acres in the heart of Rockville Centre in the vicinity of Lakeview and Hempstead Avenues. Located on high ground, the property was the best around. The site offered wide concrete sidewalks, curbs and shade trees and was a short walk to the railroad station and Clinton Avenue School. One-third of the homes, which were built of stucco or brick with tile roofs, were sold before they were built. The area became known as Cedar Terrace. It was once said of Anna Millar, "If all the real estate operators had as good ideas in artistic developments as Miss Millar, we need have no fear of the future beauty of Rockville Centre."

"If we build it, they will come" seemed to be the mantra of the moment, for soon after Millar's success, the Windsor Land and Improvement Company of New York developed the two areas between Merrick Road and Foxhurst Avenue and Lincoln Avenue and Long Beach Road. The developers declared, "The inconvenience usually annexed to the establishment of developments such as Rockville Centre Terrace and Marion Park was avoided on account of their wonderful location within Rockville Centre."

Perhaps the most popular, extensively advertised and distinctive development in the village was Canterbury Estates. On what was once wooded land lying between North Village and Hempstead Avenues stands a pretty community of homes embodying many types of architecture, including the English Tudor that gave the area its name. Each home was instrumental in presenting a picture that is at once different and beautiful. All the streets and sidewalks were paved with concrete. Its main thoroughfare winds in and out, while its side streets branch prettily from its edges. Trees abound due to the sensitivity of the builders in clearing the original land, moving only sufficient trees to allow for the building of roads and the constructing of homes.

Not everyone, however, was enamored of all this development and, dare we say, gentrification. Its many pundits were heard to say, "One week an open field is seen somewhere in the village. The next week it is laid out in streets and a dozen foundations for new houses have been started." Frances Patten Raynor Mullady said it best in her poem "Nostalgia": "Where is the place where I was born? It seems to be completely gone. Buildings and streets that I once knew have all but disappeared from view. The little brooks that graced the town are gurgling darkly underground. Places where I played and grew surely aren't the ones I knew." That may be true, my lady; however, these new neighborhoods do form the historic districts for today's generation. Let us hope they are better protectors and preservationists of Rockville Centre's HERitage and HIStory than those of yore.

To provide the necessary goods and services to this growing population, the already booming business district was also growing, thanks to John T. Davison. Davison had an extraordinary gift for envisioning the commercial, industrial and general development of the village. It was Davison who built the first modern business establishment on Village Avenue and later became instrumental in building the Bank of Rockville Centre Trust Company and the United Estates Building. However, it was as the "father of Park Avenue" that he was best known for his building and development enterprises. Davison built eleven stores and business establishments along that thoroughfare.

With Park Avenue now part of the shopping district, the village's residents had a wide variety of stores from which to choose. Even the most discerning shoppers were able to find high-quality merchandise to purchase from all the new merchants opening for business and offering top-notch customer service.

On Park Avenue were Thomas H. Darling's insurance agency, Mrs. E. Lawrence's Artistic Millinery Shop, Louis Young's delicatessen, Stanley Nestri's tailor shop, Westbrook's Candy and Ice Cream Store and George Lockitts's Sons Food Market. Along Merrick Road, shoppers could find Cohen's Department Store, the Henry P. Wahle Grocery, Manning the Jeweler, Anker's Florist and Stark and Sterrit,

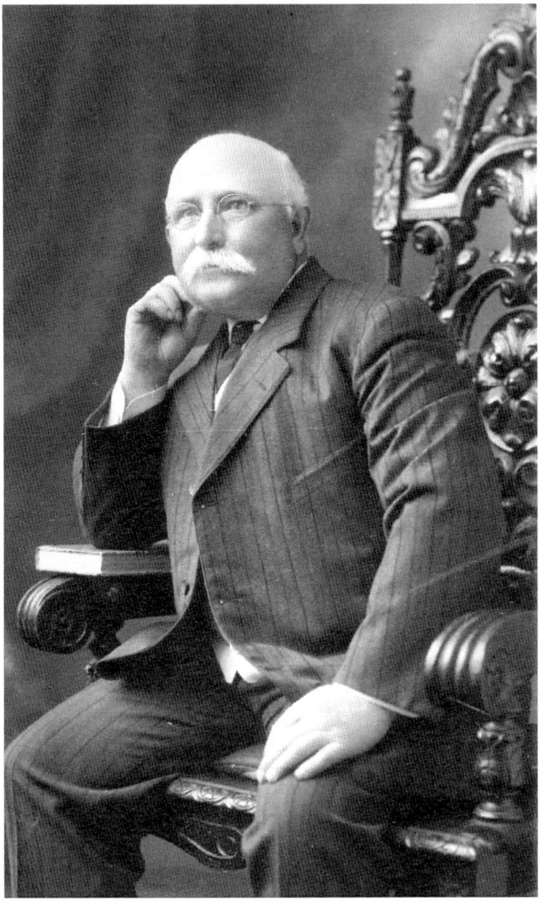

John T. Davison, the "father of Park Avenue," was responsible for building many of the stores and businesses along that thoroughfare.

a drugstore and local landmark on the corner of Merrick Road and Village Avenue.

One of the most popular stores to open was owned by George Stratigos, the grandfather of State Senator Dean Skelos. It opened as George's Pastry Shop on Park Avenue; later, it would move to Sunrise Highway, where people from miles around would stand in line holding numbered tickets. The line was so long that some of the customers would go to Mass, come back and it still would not be their turn. At one point, there were fifty employees, including Skelos and all the other grandchildren.

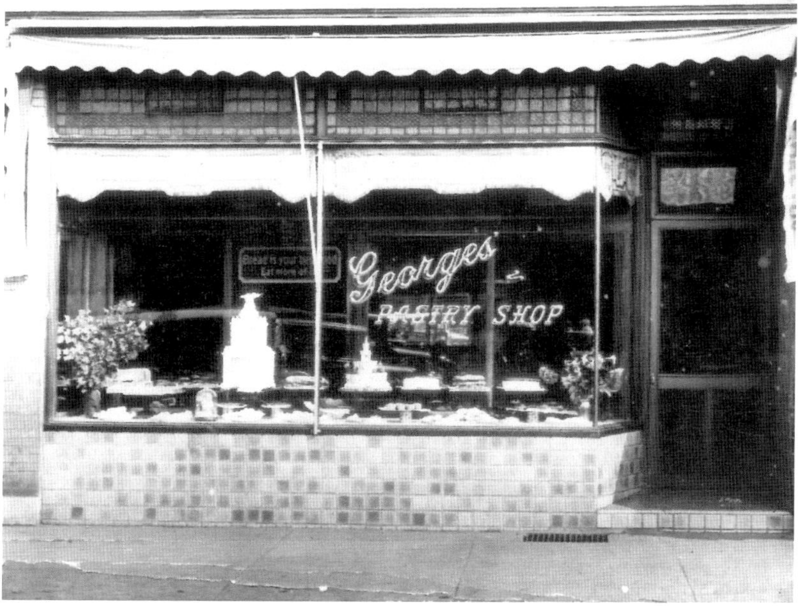

George's Pastry Shop, originally on Park Avenue, was owned by George Stratigos. The shop was later moved to Sunrise Highway. *Courtesy of Polly Vanich.*

Many of these new merchants were of the Jewish faith. They lived above their stores so they would be close to both their families and places of business. Lazarus Leder, his wife Rachel and their two young children came to Rockville Centre from Butte, Montana. Lazarus opened a custom tailoring shop on one side of Village Avenue, and Rachel started Leder's Bazaar on the other side. Leder's Bazaar was in business for fifty years. Today, the store at that location is Leder's Jewelry Store.

Louis Aronson opened a department store on Village Avenue, and Nathan Cohen operated a clothing and shoe store on Sunrise Highway. Joining them were Philip Goldberg, who dealt in wholesale liquors, and Joseph Elias, a dealer in plate glass. These men and their families formed the Nassau Hebrew Congregation and built a shul on Windsor Avenue.

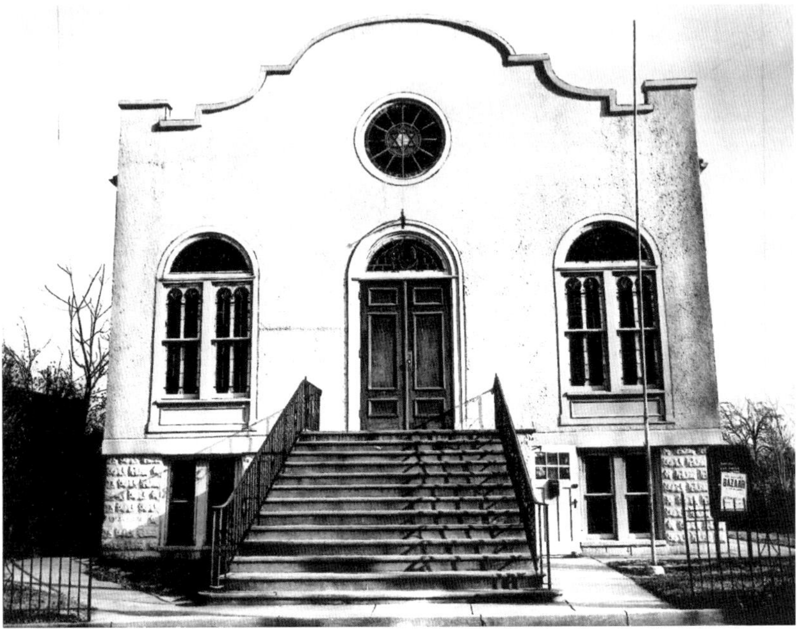

The Nassau Hebrew congregation's shul, built in 1914 on Windsor Avenue. The congregation eventually grew into Temple B'Nai Shalom, dedicated in 1949.

The women of the congregation started a sisterhood, with Mary Stavenhagen as the president. The group met in one another's homes and, later, at the shul to conduct their meetings. As the congregation grew, the ladies did their diligent duty in every way to help support their synagogue and provide a teacher for their Hebrew school. This shul eventually grew into Temple B'Nai Shalom, now located at the corner of Hempstead and Lakeview Avenues.

While coal was king during the Industrial Revolution, Rockville Centre had its own queen of coal, Mrs. M.M. Cahill, the owner, president and general manager of the Long Island Fuel Corporation. She built it into a strong, reliable, workable organization. The corporation consisted of coal companies in Rockville Centre, Lynbrook, Freeport and Laurelton. Cahill weathered a coal strike lasting six months. She once said of the corporation, "The quality of its coal cannot be excelled, and it is always the policy of the corporation to educate and help those tackling the unruly furnace for the first time."

Another large industry hatched on Maple Avenue, unbeknownst to passersby, existed below the stores: the Long Island Hatcheries, a kind of middleman operation for chicken breeders. Mammoth incubators were installed, and on Saturday afternoons and Tuesday mornings, twenty thousand eggs were delivered. It took twenty-one days for the hatching to occur, after which, on Mondays and Wednesdays, large shipments of live chicks were taken to the railroad station to be sent by parcel post to all parts of the United States. At this facility, at least, one need not wonder which came first, the chicken or the egg. It was always the other way around.

The purchase of an automobile by a Rockville Centre resident was a newsworthy event in the early twentieth century. A two-cylinder Maxwell was purchased by George M. Willets. Dr. Robert F. Hutcheson was making house calls in his gas buggy. Mr. and Mrs. Charles R. Davis were tooling around the village showing off their automobile. To service these newfangled conveyances, filling stations, repair shops, tire retailers and showrooms began doing business at a rapid pace. One of these was the Gardiner Garage and Motor Company on Merrick Road near Windsor Avenue, a distributor of Cole, Maxwell, Marion and Mercer. The Rockville Centre Garage was the agent for Buick, Charles E. Edwards sold Overlands, C.W. Vanderveer was the agent for the Paige-Detroit and Herbert E. Pearsall of Merrick Road advertised the Oldsmobile.

A Ford dealership opened as a small garage on Front Street and soon grew into a large showroom and parts department on Village Avenue. Trucks and light delivery cars made up 40 percent of sales. Private sales of automobiles made up the other 60 percent. The parts department was stocked with every part Ford produced, assuring owners a quick fix. It was said that if the need ever arose, the dealership could probably build a car from the wheels up.

Merrick Road and, later, Sunrise Highway became the two main thoroughfares bringing automobile enthusiasts to Rockville Centre, making it a popular place to stop. The Flagstaff Inn was a favorite place for travelers. It was run according to the English idea of service, as England was noted for its quaint hostelries. The Flagstaff's interior decorations were gathered from the four quarters of the globe. While diners waited for their deliciously prepared meals, they could transport themselves, via their imaginations, to South Africa, India or Europe.

At the corner of Merrick Road and Morris Avenue, the Knickerbocker Hotel was undergoing a complete renovation by its new owner, A.K. Martens. Two of the additions she made were a Dutch room and billiard room. The hotel offered a wide veranda, first-class cuisine and special rates for families wishing an extended stay. For the guests' comfort, the hotel offered private baths with hot and cold running water, steam heat, electric lights and telephones.

The Long Island Traction Company's trolleys ceased operation after many years of shuttling residents around the village and bringing commuters from Oceanside and Baldwin into the village to catch the trains into New York City and Brooklyn. Local attorneys also rode the trolleys into Mineola to attend court. It wasn't unusual for opposing attorneys to ride in the same car. For fifteen cents, a passenger could meet the New York City Subway at Ozone Park.

Harry B. Carter founded the Bee Bus Line and was already operating in Queens County. By taking over the trolley's routes, he was able to establish himself and his company in Nassau County. The heart of Bee Bus Line's operations was a large garage located in Rockville Centre. It covered an acre of ground and housed all the maintenance facilities, as well as office space for all personnel and management. In ten years, the Bee Bus Line had grown from 2 used buses to a fleet of over 120, including 38 deluxe parlor coach vehicles, and from a three-mile route to routes covering Long Island from one end to the other.

The Bee Bus Line became a success story unparalleled in bus transportation.

The Bank of Rockville Centre Trust Company was growing steadily due to two facts: one, it was the only bank in the immediate area; and two, the population had more than doubled. Talks began on the need for larger quarters, and an addition was built onto the rear of the original office in the DeMott Building. New fixtures were installed, including partitions and desks. The old fixtures were donated to the Incorporated Village of Rockville Centre for use in Village Hall, then located at Merrick Road and Lincoln Avenue. Soon, even larger quarters were needed, and the bank began planning for its own building. A plot of land was purchased at the corner of Village Avenue and Merrick Road. A building was erected, and the bank's new offices opened on April 24, 1909, with a reception for depositors.

Several other banks opened during this era of growth. The First National Bank of Rockville Centre opened on Sunrise Highway with $25,000 in capital. Its first officers included G. Byron Latimer, president; John H. Carl, vice-president; and Gabriel Toombs, cashier. Eventually, First National was taken over by its largest competitor, the Bank of Rockville Centre Trust Company. First National's building now houses the offices of the Diocese of Rockville Centre.

The Nassau County National Bank opened in 1917 on Front Street, a convenient location for commuters. Dr. D.N. Bulson became president of the bank in 1918 and served until his death in 1945. Bergen T. Raynor, formally of the Bank of Rockville Centre, became the cashier until retiring in 1950 at eighty years old.

In 1929, the South Shore Trust Company was founded by George W. Loft of the Loft Candy Company. The bank was located on North Village Avenue. The building has recently been restored and now houses an architect's office. These four banks grew from the old Rockville Centre Savings and Loan Association, which was the first financial institution that made Rockville Centre the premier financial center in Nassau County.

The Rockville Centre Post Office became one of the first occupants of the United Estates Building. The new office was equipped with combination lockboxes, a private office for then postmaster Oliver H. Tuthill and all the conveniences of a modern, up-to-date post office. Tuthill and his second in command, William P. Lister, who would become postmaster himself in 1920, saw the office grow from a comparatively small one into one with free home delivery twice a day.

The schools were becoming overcrowded, and more classroom space was needed. It was time for the public library to move out of the high school. On July 6, 1911, a special meeting of the school district was called to vote on the following: 1. The acceptance of an offer of Andrew Carnegie to give the sum of $10,000 for the purpose of erecting a free public library building; 2. The acceptance of an offer of John Lyon to provide a suitable site; and 3. For the purpose of authorizing an appropriation of $1,000 to be raised, levied and collected annually by a tax on the taxable property of said district for the maintenance of said library.

The proposition was unanimously carried by sixty-four votes. The cornerstone was laid on July 6, 1912, and was donated by a group of women who founded the Civic Club of Rockville Centre for the purpose of bettering the village. In December of the same year, the library building was completed, dedicated and opened. John Lyon donated the site, and Dr. Devillo N. Bulson, then president of the village, provided the charging desk. Joseph Elias contributed all the glass for the building, and the family of Robert A. Davison, one of the organizers and a trustee of the library, gave the remainder of the furnishings as a memorial.

Winona C. Martin was the first librarian to serve in the new library building, which still stands today on Clinton

Avenue, although it is no longer used as a library. Under her leadership, the Library Auxiliary—or, as it's known today, the Friends of the Rockville Centre Library—was organized. Martin also held the first children's story hour. It became so popular that Martin decided to publish a book, *Twelve Tales of King Arthur*, based on the material she used. In 1918, during World War I, Martin took a leave of absence to become a canteen worker in France under the auspices of the YMCA. Unfortunately, she was killed while a patient in the Claude Bernard Hospital in Paris during a bombing raid by the German army. She never made it to the French battlefield to serve with the American Expeditionary Forces.

Andrew Jackson MacElroy moved to Rockville Centre when he was appointed principal of Clinton Avenue School. He resigned rather abruptly after one term to start his own business as publisher and editor of the *Owl*, "Long Island's Breezy Magazine." The *Owl* would begin publication as the bulletin of the Rockville Centre Club, whose mission was to organize and provide social relations among its members and to promote their physical, mental and moral welfare. The club was located on Lincoln Avenue in the building that now houses the Masonic Temple. The club had a membership of nearly five hundred, and the property, which included a clubhouse and gymnasium, was worth $40,000.

The clubhouse had a large reception room, library, dining room and kitchen. The gymnasium was fifty feet wide and ninety feet long and was equipped with exercise apparatus and basketball, hardball and indoor tennis courts. The gymnasium was also used as an auditorium, being the largest on Long Island outside of Greater New York. At one end was a large stage with adjoining dressing rooms. In the basement were four bowling alleys, four billiard and pool tables, a locker room, showers, a dressing room and a swimming tank. The club also leased an athletic field and had teams in nearly every sport.

Eventually, the *Owl* became a promotional source for the school district, bringing much-needed publicity to the schools. It also became the bulletin for South Side High School. When the *Owl* went from being a magazine to a weekly newspaper, South Side started publishing its own bulletin called the *Breeze*, presumably in honor of the *Owl*'s tag line.

Remembering his roots in education, Andrew J. MacElroy went on to become a member and, later, president of the school board. At one meeting, MacElroy announced that he knew of a plot of land, three hundred square feet, for sale on Morris Avenue. The purchasing price was $10,000. Morris School opened during the winter of 1915–16, with Miss Josephine Johnson as head teacher.

This period also saw the election of Elsie Spelman, the first woman elected to the school board; the formation of a Mother's Club, the forerunner of today's Parent Teacher Association; and physical training in the schools. Jane Ward, a music teacher, was given an additional salary per month to supervise this physical training. Floyd B. Watson was hired to teach all high school mathematics and physics and to coach all varsity athletics, which included baseball, basketball, football and track. Up until then, the teams had been self-coached and supervised by one member of the faculty, usually the principal, who attended all the games and meets.

With no gymnasiums of their own, the schoolchildren were welcomed as junior members of the Rockville Centre Club. Elsie Spelman founded the Rockville Girl's Association, and the first girls' athletic meet was held on April 20, 1917, in the Rockville Centre Club, with two hundred girls participating. The girls were divided into two teams, the red and the green. After the first year, the meets became a school-sponsored event, and the colors were changed to red and blue to reflect the high school's colors. The meets continue to this day and have earned a place of honor in Rockville Centre life.

At a school board meeting held January 11, 1916, then high school principal William S. Covert suggested a reorganization of the school system to include a junior high school. The main objective was to reduce the number of pupils who terminated their formal schooling at the end of the eighth grade and to interest a larger number of boys and girls in academic work. Covert revealed his academic leadership by advancing the junior high school idea and securing its approval by the school board of education.

South Side Junior High School opened in September 1916, sharing space within the South Side High School's facility. Floyd C. VanEps was appointed principal. Just as South Side High School, when it opened in 1892, was the first high school on the south side of Long Island, so South Side Junior High School, when it opened, was the first of its kind in Nassau and Suffolk Counties.

World War I impacted Rockville Centre life in several ways. Andrew J. MacElroy resigned as president of the school board to enter the conflict. He joined the United States Army and, later, was transferred to the Royal Air Force of England, in which he achieved the rank of major.

With the war raging, the schools cooperated in every possible way. They instituted programs of economy, fundraising and physical fitness. All wastepaper was collected, baled and sold. A savings bank system was started for the sixth-, seventh-, eighth- and ninth-grade students; unfortunately, it was proven unsuccessful.

The Village of Rockville Centre was also feeling the effects of the Great War. The railroads were being pressed into service carrying troops and military supplies, causing a serious coal shortage. The greatest impact on the village would be to its supply of electricity. The Village Board of Trustees authorized village president Edwin G. Wright to purchase five to ten carloads of coal from a man in New York City for the sum of $8.65 per ton. When this failed to materialize, Wright was succeeded by Edwin W. Wallace, who reported an opportunity to purchase between 3,500 and 4,000 tons of coal for $6.25 per ton. The village board approved the purchase, the coal was delivered and the electric plant continued to operate, providing service to residents, schools and businesses.

The village board received a request from the United States government to supply electric power to its naval ordnance plant on Milburn Avenue in Baldwin. After the war, this facility was known as the Star Shell Plant and continued operating for many years on property adjacent to what is now the Coral House Restaurant and Caterers.

Also during the war, Liberty Bond drives were held, road improvements began and the Rockville Centre Fire Council came before the village board to request motorized firefighting apparatus. This request was approved, and several pieces of equipment were purchased.

Rockville Centre also formed the Ninety-third Company of the Home Defense Reserve Unit under the watch of New York State. The men were outfitted in uniforms, carried rifles and met once a week to drill, taking target practice at an abandoned reservoir with soldiers from Camp Mills, which was located in the Garden City–Mineola area.

Rockville Centre's religious life was also growing in the first two decades of the twentieth century. St. Agnes Parish had grown from Walter Johnson's blacksmith shop, on Centre Avenue, into the village's first schoolhouse and then into the quaintly picturesque Marble Church. Upon his arrival in Rockville Centre, the Reverend Peter Quealy found a parish eighteen years old and consisting of four hundred congregants. Reverend Quealy began to acquire property, gracing it with an ornate parochial school in the English Gothic style. The school contained ten classrooms and a spacious auditorium. It had an opening student enrollment of sixty. Just before classes began in September 1916, a teaching staff of five Dominican sisters arrived. Both the sisters and students were placed under the charge of Mother Petra, OP, the school's first principal. From the original five nuns came a very special woman, Sister Marian, who would spend seventy-three years of devoted service teaching at St. Agnes.

Pastor Quealy oversaw the building of a new rectory between the church and school. The original rectory was moved to the south side of College Place to serve as a convent for the Dominican sisters. In the meantime, Quealy built a gallery in the church, installed an organ and paid off the entire parish debt of $26,000.

In 1924, a high school was established, and by Christmas 1928, the sisters had moved into a beautiful new convent with a devotional and richly artistic chapel. Purchasing even more land, the now Monsignor Quealy set about creating plans for a new church to accommodate an increased Catholic population. The White Marble Church, partly concealed by graceful maple trees, had to make way for a more majestic edifice. On October 23, 1933, after its last Mass, demolition began on the church. Cathedral-like in quiet strength, grace and majesty, the new church's cross-crowned 150-foot tower dominated the skyline. The tower now houses the same bell that for nearly thirty years rang in the marble belfry. By building this cathedral, perhaps Monsignor Quealy was already envisioning the diocese it would become.

Although there had been a Congregationalist church in Rockville Centre prior to the 1900s, it was eventually disbanded. A new Congregationalist church was organized in 1926 with the help of the New York Association of Congregational Churches. Land was purchased and a church erected at Princeton and Morris Avenues. Its first minister was the Reverend John B. Hanna. Its first congregation was made up of families who had moved to Rockville Centre from Brooklyn.

The Presbyterian church started as a Sabbath school, meeting on Sundays at 3:00 p.m. in the Reliance Hose Company's firehouse. Shortly thereafter, a desire for a preaching service arose, and one began being held following the Sunday school sessions. The congregation would eventually erect a church at the corner of Lakeview and Morris Avenues at what was considered, at the time, to be the approximate geographical center of the village.

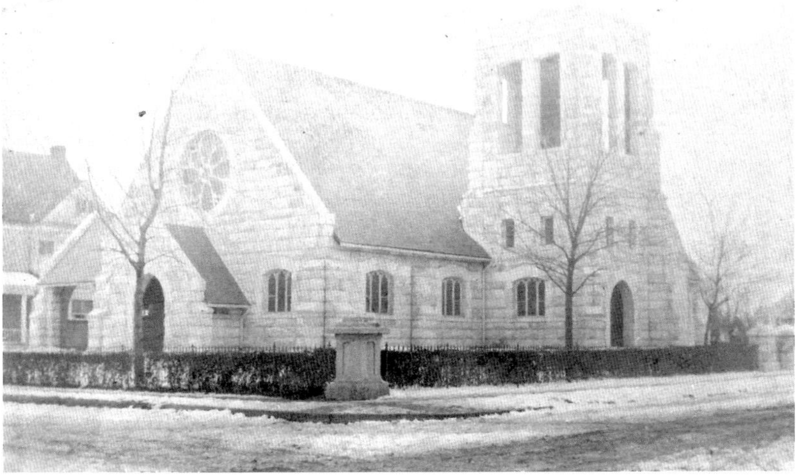

Above: The artistic and picturesque St. Agnes Marble Church was built in 1902 under the supervision of Reverend James Flood and dedicated on June 11, 1905.

Below: The old Presbyterian church at the corner of Lakeview and Morris Avenues, thought to be the geographical center of the village. *Courtesy of Rockville Centre Public Library.*

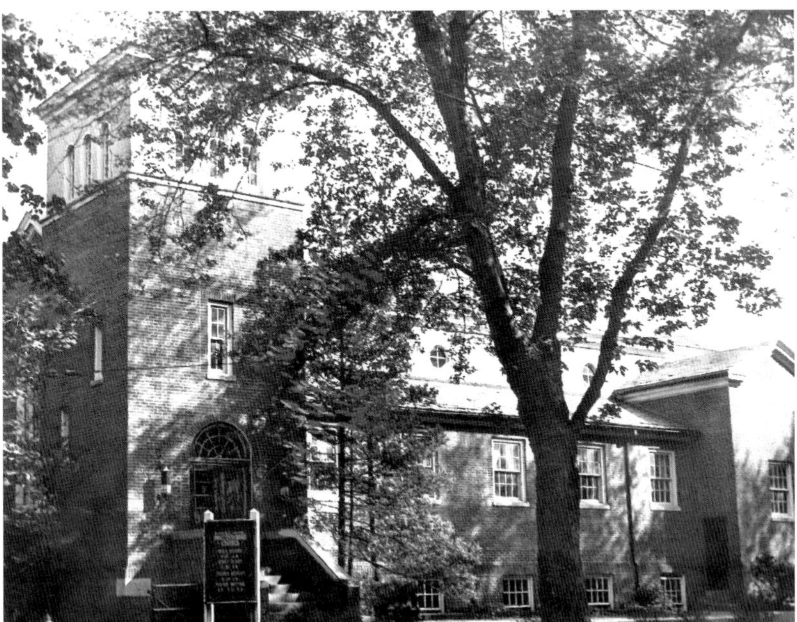

With World War I over and the first two decades of the twentieth century drawing to a close, the people of Rockville Centre were once again forming new organizations, building new facilities and creating new firsts.

American Legion Post Number 303 was founded in 1919. Helen McGrath Shannon served in World War I as a yeoman first class in the United States Navy. She was the first woman veteran to march, proudly, with the male veterans of the post.

By 1921, the legion was meeting in the Eureka Hook and Ladder Company's firehouse. A special meeting was held and a committee appointed to prepare plans and erect a building. They hoped to raise funds for the project through popular subscription. Unfortunately, not enough funds were raised, and neither the plans nor the building came to fruition.

As soon as the proposition to build a new high school was advanced, the idea of making it a memorial to those from

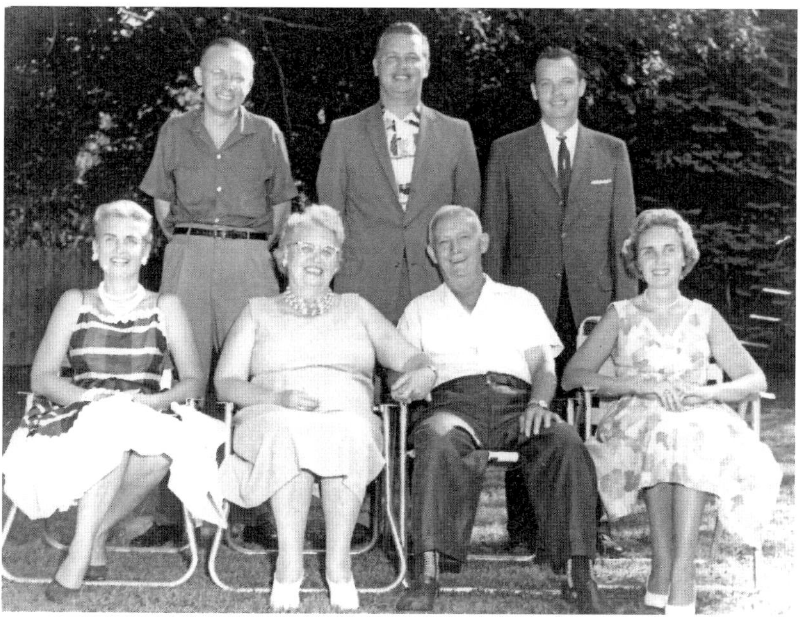

Helen McGrath Shannon (seated, second from left) served as a navy yeoman first class during World War I. *Courtesy of Patricia Odermatt.*

Rockville Centre who gave their lives in the Great War was conceived. A committee from the American Legion was given permission by the school board to plant fourteen trees as a memorial. The trees were planted in front of the school's property on Hillside Avenue. A dedication ceremony was held on Armistice Day, November 11, 1921.

By this time, the American Legion was joined by the Veterans of Foreign Wars Post 103, which also established itself as a fraternal, patriotic, historical and educational organization. On December 15, 1921, these two groups were invited to occupy quarters within the new high school. The idea was accepted by both groups. The Memorial Room, as it was called, was located on the third floor and housed many war trophies. It served as quarters for both the American Legion and the Veterans of Foreign Wars for many years, after which each group secured its own quarters.

An African American children's vacation school, held in Community Hall on Banks Avenue, came into being after a stirring appeal by Elizabeth Adams Davis, the director of religious education at St. Mark's Methodist Church. The appeal was made before the Rockville Centre Exchange Club, completely sweeping the bankers and real estate men off their feet and prompting them to open their pocketbooks. In 1926, there were fifty-seven pupils enrolled, ranging in age from four to fifteen. Davis became the school's director, with Lottie and Jean Taylor, of Westbury, as teachers. The children received instruction in Bible studies, music, storytelling, drama, carpentry, sewing and art. Classes met from 8:00 a.m. to 11:45 a.m. five days a week.

Although originally an experiment, the results achieved exceeded the highest expectations of those behind the project. The parents promised to lend their support by looking about for the means to make the school a permanent institution. At the time, it was the only such school on Long Island and one of a handful in New York State.

The suffragette movement was underway in the village, led by Edna Buckman Kearns. Kearns hitched the cause of women's suffrage to a horse-drawn wagon, in which she drove to the Mineola Fair every year. Dressed in colonial garb, Kearns would stop along the way to speak to people about the importance of giving women the right to vote. Kearns became a leader in both the New York State campaign and the national campaign. Many other women in the village also took up the cause, attending the Nassau County Assembly District Convention and Suffrage Luncheon, held by the New York State Woman Suffrage Party. It was held in the Nassau Hotel in Long Beach.

The National Prohibition Party brought its own brand of notoriety to the village when it nominated village resident William F. Varney for president of the United States at its national convention in 1928. Varney had taken up the issue of prohibition while a patient in a hospital ward after undergoing surgery. Many of the other patients in the ward were suffering the effects of alcoholism. However, the National Prohibition Party failed to qualify in its attempt to get its ticket on the ballot in all the states. Varney would later run for governor of New York State and mayor of Rockville Centre. Although unsuccessful in his political ambitions, Varney remained a prominent resident and businessman.

Dr. Hartley E. Boorum established a small private sanitarium in a former private residence at the southwest corner of Park and Lincoln Avenues. The "San," as the locals called it, was the sole medical facility available to a population of sixty-five thousand people along Nassau County's south shore.

The newly formed Nassau County Medical Society issued a report suggesting the construction of a hospital in the vicinity of Rockville Centre. Mary Pearson, a registered nurse and superintendent of the sanitarium, teamed up with George D.A. Combes when he became director of the San after Boorum's death. Together, they began a dialogue for the creation of United South Side Communities Hospital. On December 16, 1926, articles of incorporation were drawn up and signed. The hospital was erected on a seven-acre parcel of land in the southeast area of Rockville Centre on Oceanside Road. South Nassau Communities Hospital opened in 1928.

Predating South Nassau Communities Hospital, Mercy Hospital was founded by the Nursing Sisters of the Sick and Poor in a wood frame structure in Hempstead. Property was purchased in 1917; however, it wasn't until 1939 that ground was broken in Rockville Centre for the new Mercy Hospital, with a capacity for seventy-five patient beds. By 1941, all of the patients had been moved from Hempstead to Mercy Hospital's new facility on Mill Road adjoining the Southern State Parkway.

Lest anyone think Rockville Centre's residents were all work and no play, nothing could be further from the truth. The old abandoned reservoir on the east side of the village, affectionately known as the "Dry Rez," became a recreational center for both children and adults. The area included open

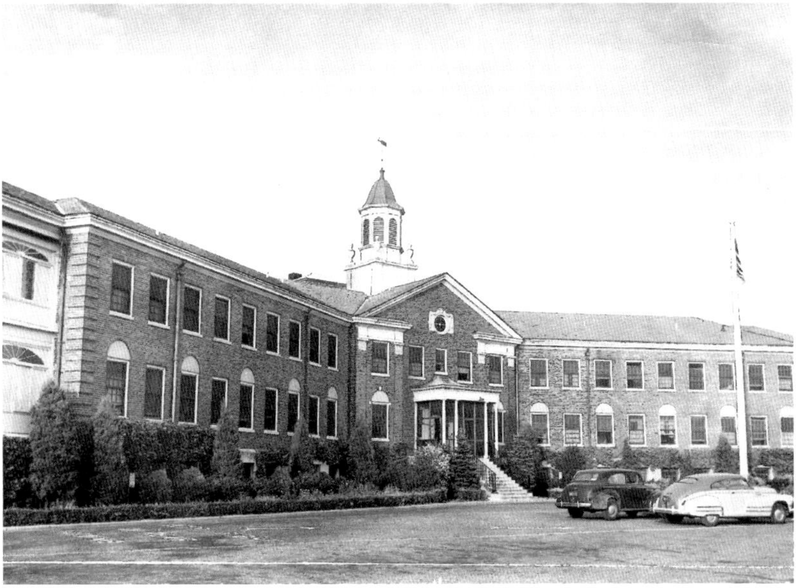

South Nassau Communities Hospital opened on December 16, 1926. It was founded by businessman George D.A. Combes and registered nurse Mary Pearson.

fields on which to play baseball and other sports and to welcome the circus when it came to town. A pond at the eastern end of the property served as a place to swim in the summer and ice skate in the winter. The snow-covered mounds surrounding the reservoir provided an exciting sledding experience for the more adventurous among the residents.

Another group of adventurers found a new use for the area. In 1928, Bert Shields, a former Royal Canadian Air Force pilot, spotted the eighty-acre field from the sky. After receiving permission from the village to use the field for the promotion of aviation and to teach young people how to fly, Shields and his twenty-pilot Sunrise Flying Club set to work. They cleared enough scrub brush to create a runway eight hundred feet in length to permit takeoff and landing. The club also purchased a two-seat, open-cockpit, fabric-covered plane with an OX-5 engine. The airfield at Rockville Centre opened on August 19, 1928, at 3:00 p.m., and Assemblyman Edwin W. Wallace was heard to say, "I expect to use the air service between Rockville Centre and Albany when the legislature convenes." Also officiating at the opening ceremonies were village mayor Charles C. Richmond; Sanford A. Davison, president of the Nassau County Bar Association; and, of course, Bert Shields.

Actress Rae Powell christened the Sunrise Flying Club's first plane the New Moon, the name of her Broadway musical. Shields took the actress and village resident Sarah Davison Leukins for a ride in the plane. Someone suggested flying the plane upside down. "No, no!" yelled the actress. "Yes, yes!" yelled Sarah. Unfortunately, it is not recorded who won that debate.

In May 1929, another plane was christened by Helen Eely of Freeport, a well-known aviatrix. She christened the plane the Flying Venus. Also on the program that day were flying stunts performed by Bert Shields, a parachute jump by William Knaust of Roosevelt Field and rides taken by 110 spectators.

Two young boys from the village impressed by these flying machines managed to gain the attention of the aviators. The first was Hartley S. Grim, who watched the flights from the front porch of his parents' home. His curiosity was piqued, and he reasoned that if he gained the friendship of the flying club's dog, he would gain the trust of the aviators. It worked; he spent many hours at the field doing chores. Soon he was rewarded with a flight in the club's shuttle from Rockville Centre to Curtis Field, now Green Acres Shopping Center.

Ronnie Storz was the other young boy. He cleaned the planes using towels from his mother's linen closet. He, too, was rewarded for his efforts with a flight to either Roosevelt Field in Garden City or Curtis Field in Valley Stream. His mother found out about the flight, and pointing skyward, she yelled, "What are you doing up there?"

Today, the area is home to the John A. Anderson Recreation Center and a neighborhood of homes known as Greystone, built from the gray granite of the reservoir.

Another recreation area popular in the 1920s with village residents was Hempstead Lake State Park. It consisted of another abandoned reservoir of the Brooklyn Water Works and the superintendent's house, which was split in half and moved to other locations. One half now serves as a residence on Hempstead Avenue; it's not clear where the other half was moved. Also, the filter beds were flooded, allowing for ice skating in winter. Eventually, it was turned into the model boat basin.

The area became a popular picnic spot, especially for school outings. The woods in their natural state were very beautiful, and a dirt wagon path ran around the lake. In 1926, Hempstead Lake State Park was formed, adding twenty-six miles of bridle paths winding around the lake and through the woods. Stables were built just north of where Mercy Hospital is now located. On Sundays, groups of young people would ride off the beaten paths along undeveloped roads and lanes as far as Freeport. One of those riders, Margaret Phelps Hopkins, who later became a village historian and archivist at the Museum of Rockville Centre and is now deceased, wrote

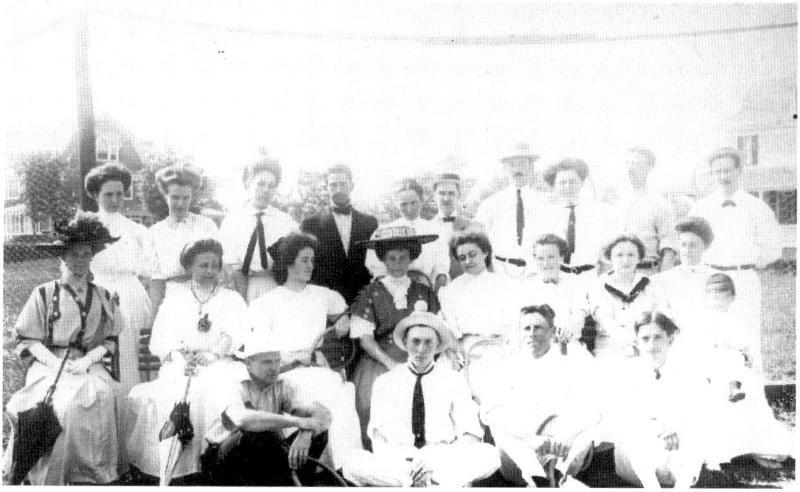

The Rockville Centre Tennis Club. Among its members was the actor John Barrymore. They played on courts at the corner of Maple and Morris Avenues.

in a 1993 personal memoir, "The horses enjoyed straying as much as the riders did."

Tennis courts, athletic fields, children's playgrounds, an archery range and a miniature golf course were also added. In 1931, a hand-painted, covered carousel, donated by August Hecksher to the State of New York, became a permanent part of the park.

The Rockville Centre Tennis Club, made up of both men and women, welcomed the actor John Barrymore, a summer resident, to the club. The tennis courts were located at the corner of Morris and Maple Avenues, the site now occupied by a firehouse. Barrymore and village resident Chloe Skilton were among the top players, winning the Mixed Doubles Championship in 1912.

Golfers, too, were seeking their own club and course. On October 28, 1923, the Rockville Country Club, affectionately dubbed the "Links," opened on what was once farmland between Long Beach Road and DeMott Avenue. Hiram R.

Smith, former president of the Bank of Rockville Centre Trust Company and by then supervisor of the town of Hempstead, presided over the dedication ceremony. Smith urged in his speech that in promoting the new club, it be made a civic and social center for the village and not just a golf club. Golf enthusiasts are still playing on the eighteen-hole course, and many social events take place within its clubhouse.

Firemen's tournaments and parades were another form of sportsmanship. The first of these was held on Labor Day, September 1, 1911, along Observer Street, now Sunrise Highway. This location was due, in part, to its being one hundred feet wide and having a level, firmly compacted roadbed. The tournament included a tug-of-war, won by the Reliance team, defeating the Live Oak team by seven inches. There were also three-legged races, sack races, one-hundred-yard dashes, broad and high jump contests, relay races and individual ladder climbing and hose contests. After the tournament, a parade took place, winding its way through the village, starting from fire headquarters on Washington Street and ending on Village Avenue, where the paraders were inspected and all the prizes won during the day were given out.

Today, the village hosts many firemen's parades both on the local and the state level. Rockville Centre's bravest now hold their tournaments on Firemen's Field, adjacent to the South Side High School's property off Shepard Street. The property was once known as Bennett's Grove, and beautiful dogwood trees graced the area. Among the stands of trees stood Camp Nuhn, owned and operated by its namesake, John H. Nuhn. Both the Girl Scouts and Boy Scouts held their jamborees at the camp.

Scouting is still an important part of village life. One of its proudest moments came when Arthur Rose Eldred became the first Eagle Scout in America after earning the twenty-one merit badges required. Eldred became interested in scouting through his brother Hubert W. Eldred, who formed Boy Scout Troop One in Rockville Centre. The troop was

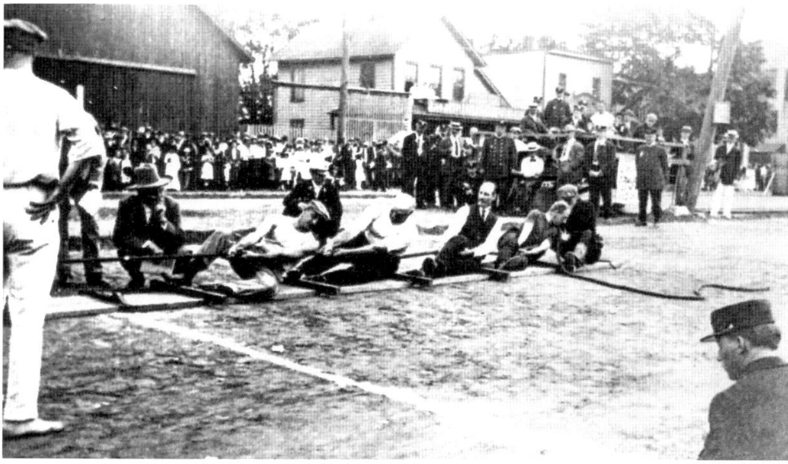

The first firemen's tournament was held on Monday, September 1, 1911. It took place on Observer Street, now Sunrise Highway.

so well uniformed and well drilled that it was invited to New York City as part of an honor guard for General Robert S. Bader Powell, the founder of the Boy Scout movement. After graduating from Cornell University, Eldred moved to New Jersey, where he continued his interest in the Boy Scouts, living long enough to witness his own son, Willard, receive his Eagle Scout designation.

Several motion picture and vaudeville theaters brought entertainment to the village residents. The Magnet Theatre opened on the northwest corner of Park Avenue and Sunrise Highway. It hosted two shows nightly and Saturday matinees. The Strand Theater opened on Sunrise Highway with four vaudeville acts and two features: *The Ruling Passion* and *A Pair of Kings*, a comedy. All 1,035 seats with leather cushions and backs were on the main floor. There was a cooling and heating system that sent forced air through mushroom ventilators. In summer, iced air was sent through the system, the forerunner of today's air conditioning. Music to accompany the silent films was supplied by an organ and orchestra. The Strand was also the site of the first DeForest talking picture shown on

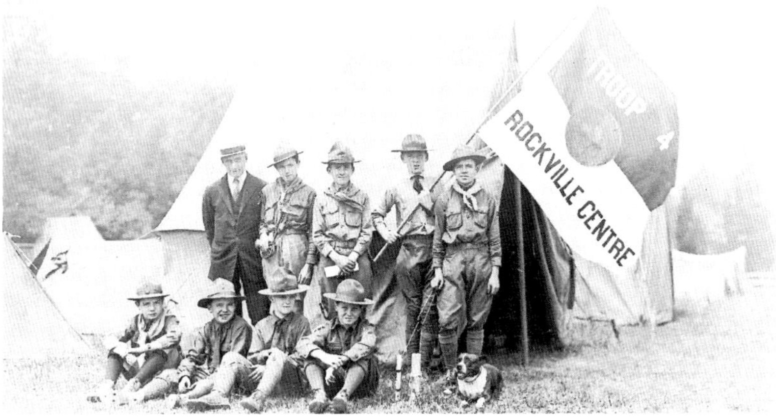

Although not a member of Troop 4, pictured here, Arthur R. Eldred became the first Eagle Scout in America, earning the twenty-one badges required.

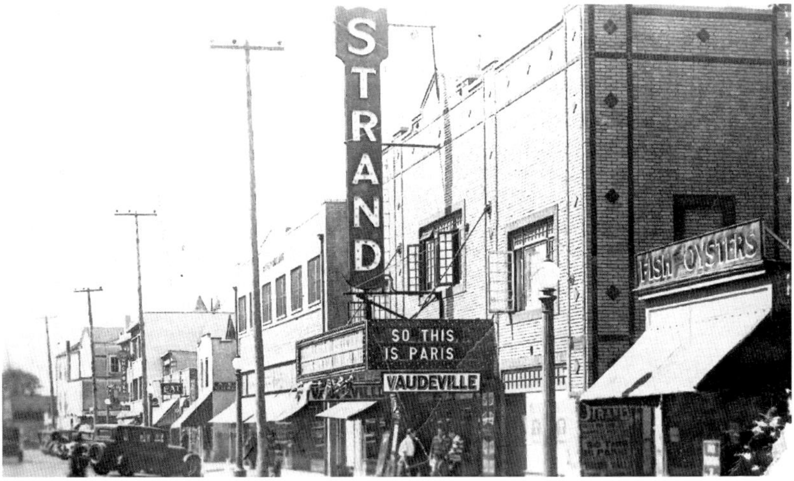

In 1922, the Strand Theater opened with four vaudeville acts, a feature film starring George Arliss and the comedy *A Pair of Kings*.

Long Island. A big box, like a radio, and large speakers were mounted to the back wall of the theater.

On the property once owned by Alexander Davison on the corner of Merrick Road and Park Avenue, a new theater was built. A contest, open to all village residents, was held to find a name for the new enterprise. A young girl won the contest with the name the Fantasy, which it is still called today. The theater was housed in a Moorish-style building that hosted many motion picture parties, some of which were held on New Year's Eve. One such party drew a capacity crowd to see two feature films, one with Evelyn Prentice, William Powell and Myrna Loy and the other starring Joe E. Brown.

During the Depression, audiences were wooed by dish nights, when glass dishes were given away with the price of admission. Most of the dishes, unfortunately, shattered as forgetful audiences rose to leave. This is how Depression

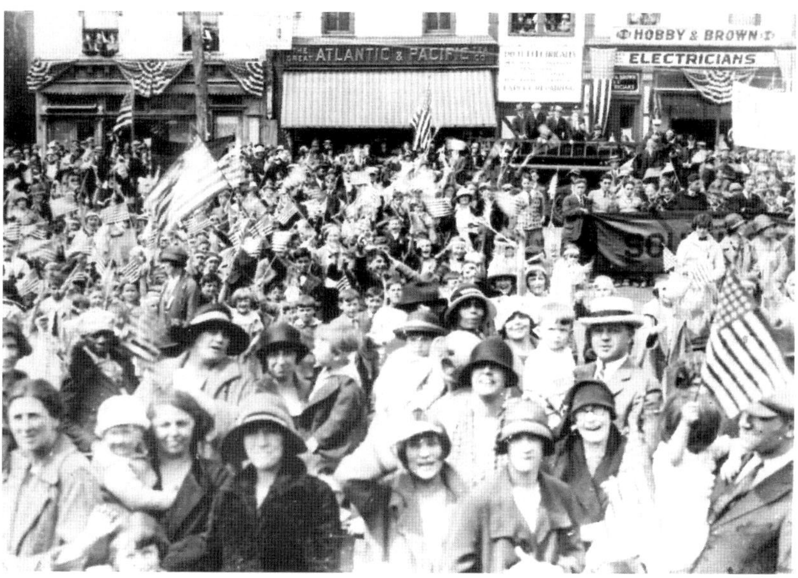

Rockville Centre residents awaiting the arrival of the first electric railroad train between Pennsylvania Station in New York City and Babylon in 1926.

glass collectables got its name. Today, this glassware is highly prized for its many patterns and colors.

The people of Rockville Centre turned out in droves to see the first electric train between the village and Babylon pull into the station on Wednesday, May 23, 1925. Schools were let out, and all the children were given small American flags to wave. Everyone was invited to board the train, either at Pennsylvania Station in Manhattan or at their home station, for a free ride out to Babylon, the last stop. They could then board another train to return them to Rockville Centre.

As Rockville Centre's greatest growth period began to wind down, its residents were looking toward the future conservatively, hoping that in ten years Rockville Centre would be experiencing an even more wondrous time and that the village would become an even more wondrous beauty spot, with an even more fascinating group of home-loving folk with the same characteristics as those who had come before—people who have an honesty of purpose, a sincerity of conviction and a loyalty to keeping the home fires burning. Little did they know how great that loyalty would need to be.

Chapter 5

LIFE INTERRUPTED

The Great Depression took its toll throughout the village. The building boom of the 1920s had slowed to a snail's pace, and its halcyon days were waning. Just as it is in today's great recession, white-collar jobs were the first to go, and since a large percent of village residents held these jobs, things did not bode well for Rockville Centre.

Those who had invested in the stock market lost most, if not all, the money they had put in. Oddly enough, there was one resident, John F. Vogel, who was still purchasing stocks in the Goodyear Tire and Rubber Company, General Motors and the Radio Corporation of America. Apparently Vogel was astute enough to realize that this, too, shall pass.

Others, however, found this to be too risky, especially since many of the car dealerships and other ancillary businesses of the automobile industry were going belly up. The only businesses that were surviving were the mechanics' shops and filling stations. This was due to the fact that people were holding on to their cars for longer periods of time and cutting back on driving instead of giving up driving entirely. Retail stores were also having trouble surviving. The once bustling business district was filled with vacant stores, and what was once the place for residents to meet and greet one another declined as the center of life.

Many residents were losing their homes to foreclosure; they were taken over by the government's Home Owners Loan Corporation. Those who were still fortunate to have a steady income could buy these homes at drastically reduced prices after a lengthy application and bidding process.

The employees of the village accepted a 5 percent cut in salary, and the police department received numerous applications from the unemployed seeking positions as patrolmen. The salary at the time was fifty dollars per week, half of what these former white-collar workers were used to earning.

The village created a relief fund, enlisting volunteers from the public. One of these volunteers was James E. Stiles, founder of the *Nassau Daily Review*, Long Island's first daily newspaper, headquartered in Rockville Centre. Stiles used his editorials to publicize the fund and also negotiated a 10 percent cut in salary from his employees.

William J. Murray, along with other residents and clergy, also worked tirelessly on behalf of the relief fund. Before coming to Rockville Centre, Murray had been involved in many fields of endeavor, including publishing, insurance, politics and civil service. Once here, he was on the rosters of many organizations relating to church, education, banking and charity. Throughout his many years of community service, Murray served on the Rockville Centre Public Library Board of Trustees for sixteen years and as postmaster from August 11, 1939, to May 31, 1954. Former mayor Eugene J. Murray continues his father's work through the Rockville Centre Community Fund, which today provides for residents in need of fuel, rent, clothing, food and compassion.

Rockville Centre's schools faced a challenge when Nassau County could not borrow enough monies to cover the tax revenues usually sent to them and the other school districts within the county. After being chosen to represent all the school districts, John H. Scott, president of Rockville Centre's

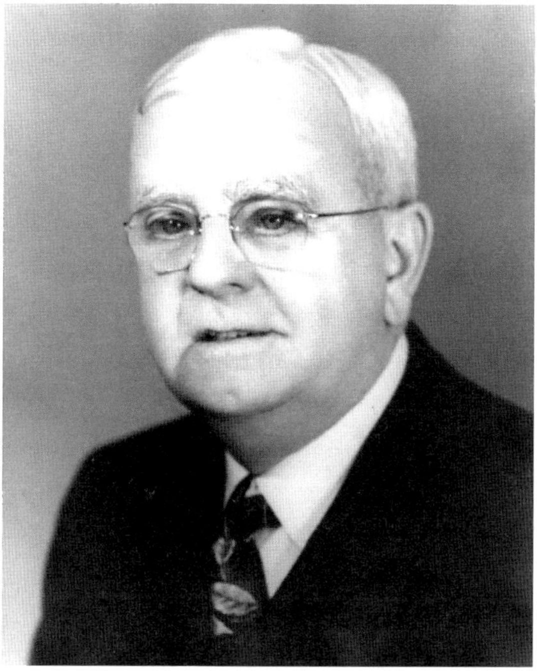

William J. Murray served on the library board and as postmaster. During the Depression, he helped raise funds for those in need.

school board, sent this reply to the county: if the schools had to close or curtail their work, a letter would be sent home to the parents of every pupil. The letter would advise the parents that the monies were being held up because of the county's refusal to live up to the law. Soon after, the monies due to the school districts were forthcoming.

All school employees' salaries were cut by 5 percent due to the Depression. People began to resent the many female teachers whose husbands were employed, so the board of education passed a resolution to the effect that any female teachers who were married would not be reengaged the following year. Unbelievable!

Not everything was gloom and doom. Work projects were being set up. One was the lot and block project, funded by Nassau County. It involved a massive changeover in the county's file of taxable properties. Many of Rockville Centre's unemployed men worked on it.

Nassau County also had an art project spearheaded by Rockville Centre resident William F. Waltemath. The federal Works Progress Administration (WPA) was also seeking employment for artists who had difficulty finding private commissions. Schools were advised that they could commission murals and oil paintings prepared by well-qualified artists for only the cost of materials used. The Rockville Centre Board of Education took advantage of these projects by commissioning a six-panel mural depicting the purchase of land from the Native Americans, an early country schoolhouse, the coming of the first railroad train to the village and the first South Side High School. Under the WPA, two oil paintings were commissioned, one of Jennie E. Hewitt, a most beloved teacher, and the other of school superintendent William S. Covert. The former was to be hung in Hewitt Elementary School and the latter in the Board of Education Room.

Although the housing market was declining, there was one bright spot when Abraham Levitt, who had already purchased one hundred plots of land in Rockville Centre as an investment, was able to sell many of them to speculative builders. A total of 40 houses were in various stages of construction when one of the builders went out of business, reverting the land back to Levitt. Experiencing difficulties himself, Levitt was joined by his sons William and Alfred, forming what would become a very successful and profitable family enterprise. In 1932, the Levitts purchased more land and constructed another 250 homes in the area known as Strathmore. The houses were built in the half-timbered style popular in Rockville Centre. Today these homes are affectionately called Levitt Tudors by the residents.

As the second half of the 1930s was getting underway, several other bright spots were popping up to bolster the spirits of Rockville Centre's citizenry. Central Synagogue of Nassau County was organized in 1935, when William Godnick gathered a congregation of friends, inspiring them with the challenge of Reform Judaism. On February 13,

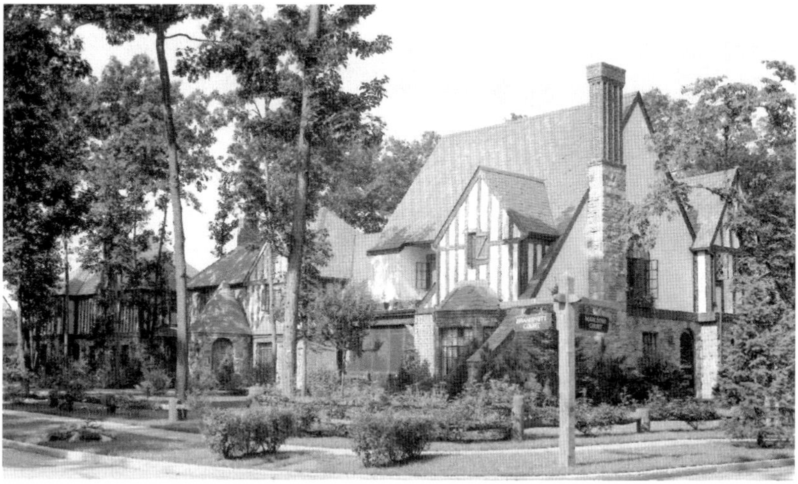

Abraham Levitt and Sons developed the area known as Strathmore. Pictured is one of the Levitt Tudors, as they are called by the locals.

1936, the congregation held its first Sabbath service in Edith McIntosh's music studio.

During that same year, several events took place. A religious school opened with an enrollment of thirty children under the aegis of Bertha Godnick, a women's organization was formed with thirty members, the congregation was officially incorporated with William Godnick as president, Roland B. Gittlesohn was engaged as rabbi and the first High Holy Day service was held in the Masonic Temple on Lincoln Avenue on September 17.

On October 29, 1941, under the leadership of Sydney W. Roos, the DeMott Avenue property was acquired for the proposed synagogue. However, World War II interrupted the building program. In 1945, the congregation was looking forward to an influx of postwar membership, and the building resumed. The synagogue was completed on September 9, 1949.

The aforementioned music studio of Edith McIntosh was originally located in the Nassau Daily Review Building on Sunrise Highway. Eventually, McIntosh moved her studio into

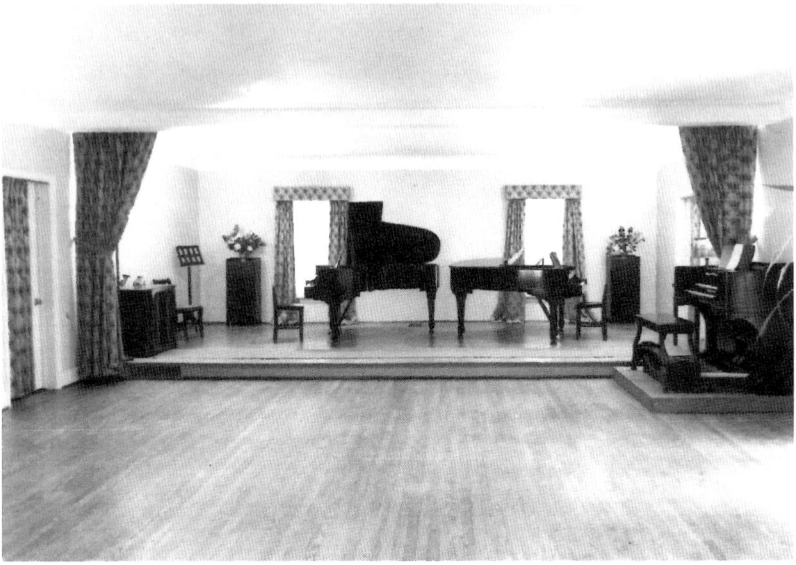

Edith McIntosh's music studio, the scene of many elementary and advanced piano recitals and community meetings. *Courtesy of Laura and James Hennig.*

her home on Hillside Avenue, continuing to teach elementary and advanced piano playing, harmony, counterpoint and orchestration. McIntosh continued her affiliation with the *Nassau Daily Review* by becoming the newspaper's music editor. She graciously opened her studio to many organizations for meetings and programs. She also opened her studio to the public for her students' recitals, which were always popular and well received.

In 1937, the Reverend Morgan M. Days came to Rockville Centre as pastor of the Shiloh Baptist Church, a wood structure with a congregation of 180. In 1945, a new church building was erected on North Centre Avenue. By that time, the congregation had grown to 1,500, with six chairs, three usher boards and seven auxiliary boards. Reverend Days launched a campaign to finish and furnish the interior of the church. He received strong support from all sectors of the village, and all the other religious denominations contributed $33,000 and many hours of their time and talents.

Reverend Days demonstrated his concern for all people and for just causes everywhere. He served for twelve years as the chairman of the village's Human Rights Commission. Reverend Days was honored by President Harry S Truman for his contributions to race relations in Nassau County and by Governor Nelson D. Rockefeller for his years of outstanding service to Rockville Centre. In March 1980, Reverend Days was invited to the White House by President Jimmy Carter to discuss community, state and national affairs. Like the Reverend Mordecai Rock Smith, Reverend Morgan M. Days became a popular leading citizen of his day.

As the 1930s drew to a close and the war years were on the horizon, women were once more at the forefront of activity. A national honor came to Rockville Centre resident Doris Corwith of American Legion Post #303 when she was elected president of the National American Legion Auxiliaries.

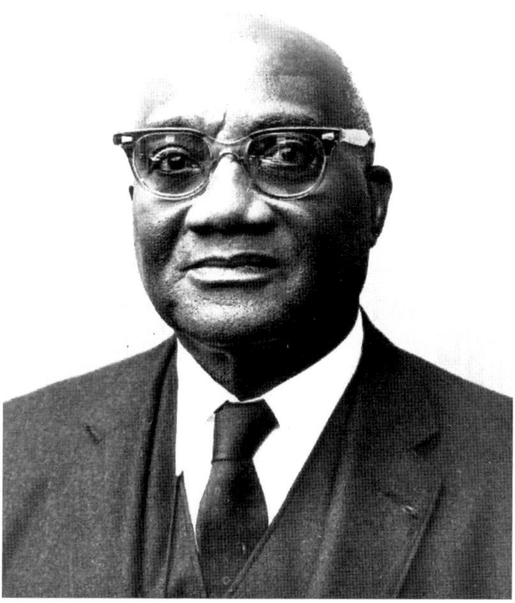

Reverend Morgan M. Days, first pastor of Shiloh Baptist Church, was cited by President Harry S Truman for his notable contributions to race relations.

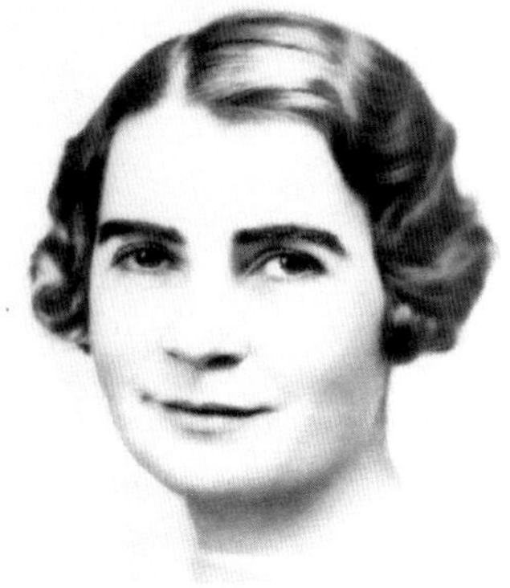

A national honor came to Rockville Centre when Doris Corwith was elected national president of the American Legion Auxiliary in 1939.

Corwith had previously served as chairwoman of both the Nassau County and New York State American Legion Auxiliaries. She also worked for the National Broadcasting Company for over twenty years.

The Nassau Woman's Club was founded on March 9, 1939, and began meeting for discussions on how best to organize and promote subjects of philanthropic and cultural importance. Its members also discussed how the club could become an important factor in the community. Mrs. William Reblen was the first president, and meetings were held in members' homes. As membership grew, the club held its general meetings in various locations, such as the Coral House in Baldwin and the Lincoln Inn, the American Legion Hall and the Republican Club, all in Rockville Centre. Today, the club meets at the United Church of Rockville Centre on Morris Avenue.

During World War II, the Nassau Woman's Club set up a Defense Committee to assign its members duties and activities at the USO centers at Fort Hamilton in Brooklyn and Mitchel Field, an air base spread out between the communities of Uniondale, Garden City and East Meadow. The Red Cross workroom was set up after a request made to the mayor and Village Board of Trustees to use the Station Pump House on Long Beach Road was approved. Many hours were put in by the women of Rockville Centre, sewing, rolling bandages and pursuing other war-related activities.

In August 1941, an extensive program of Red Cross training courses was offered. The courses included first aid; nurses' aides; nutrition; canteen work; motor mechanics; arts and skills; and staff assistants. Applicants were asked to register with Mrs. Dwight T. Bonham, chairwoman of the Rockville Centre Branch of the Red Cross. Over 150 women responded and registered. The Red Cross Woman's Motor Corps was formed and began transporting nurses, nurses' aides, the women of the Arts and Skills Committee headed by Mrs. Gay McFarland and other volunteers to and from the veterans' hospitals. The women were much in demand and put in countless hours seeing to the needs of returning veterans. The Arts and Skills Committee provided

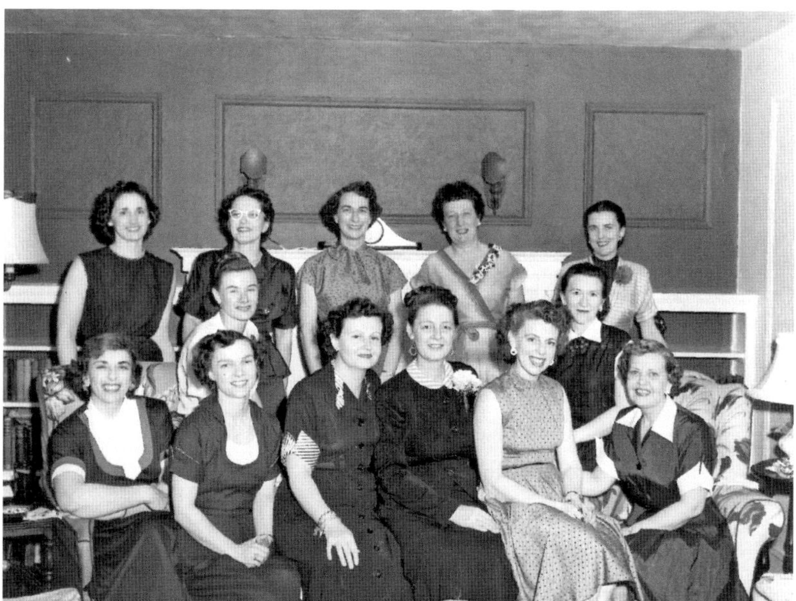

The Nassau Woman's Club was founded on March 7, 1939, meeting in members' homes. The club remains a philanthropic organization to this day.

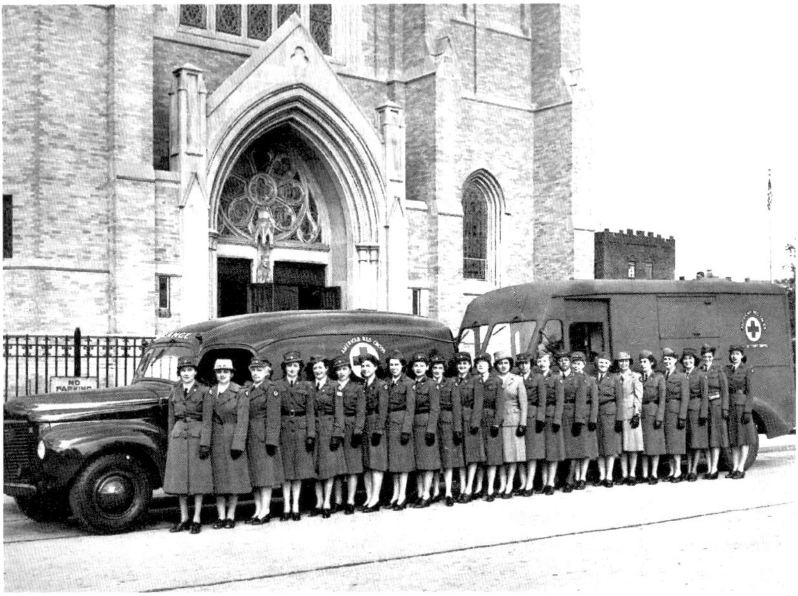

The Rockville Centre Red Cross Woman's Motor Corps was formed in 1941. The female volunteers were trained as drivers and mechanics.

occupational therapy, retraining the veterans for their return to civilian life.

Women also played leading roles in the British Relief Office located on Sunrise Highway (later moving to Front Street), the Woman's War Activities Committee of the Rockville Centre Civilian Protection Unit and war bond drives and rallies.

Rockville Centre's residents faced the rationing of tires, gasoline, home heating oil, food and other consumer goods. Although tires were the first to be rationed, gasoline rationing began in May 1942. Cards were issued in all the elementary schools, and the teachers were pressed into service to carry out all the government-sponsored rationing programs. Gasoline could not be purchased without a card. To obtain one, the applicants had to bring their vehicle registration certificates to the schools.

The schools also participated in the war effort by holding drills for the protection of both students and all school

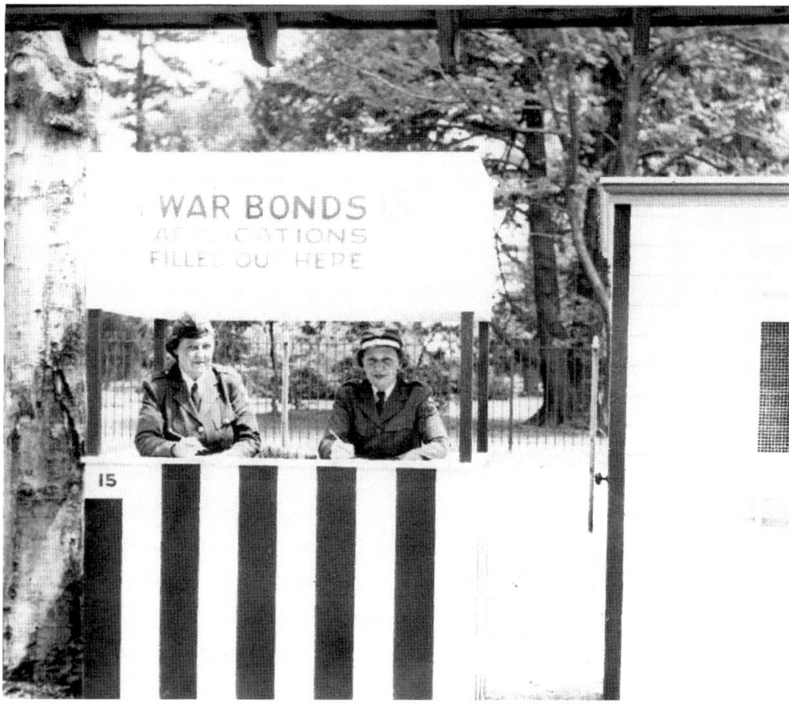

A war bond rally was held on August 26, 1942. Shown are Florence Lloyd and Gladys Shannon at a booth, ready to sign up applicants.

personnel. The students were instrumental in carrying out the salvage, thrift and war savings programs. School employees were subject to a victory tax of 5 percent of their gross salaries, which was collected by the schools and forwarded to the collector of internal revenue. All evening programs for adults were suspended to conserve fuel, light and power.

Some of the South Side High School boys wished to enlist in the armed forces before graduation. To accommodate them, the board of education passed a resolution granting high school seniors full credit toward graduation for subjects in which they were doing satisfactory work at the time of enlistment. Many young men took advantage of this opportunity and earned their high school diplomas while away from South Side High.

There was still a lot of vacant land in the village, and due to the rationing of food, these large plots of land were parceled out to residents wishing to plant victory gardens. Home heating oil was also becoming scarce, and coal was once again a marketable commodity. Some enterprising homeowners were driving to Long Beach to gather driftwood to burn in their fireplaces.

The fire department reported that 127 of its members were in the armed forces, and an appeal went out for temporary members to help maintain service. In addition, 100 citizens volunteered to help the police force to assure residents they need not worry about possible wartime attempts to damage facilities that were vital to public health and safety. The 100 volunteers were trained and disciplined in defense procedures. These men and women were members of the Rockville Centre Defense Unit, under the direction of W. Harry Lister, and were ready to respond to any emergency. After the war, these World War II responders formed the Rockville Centre Auxiliary Police.

The Civil Defense Unit was headquartered in the basement of the Tudor Apartments at the corner of Hempstead and Village Avenues, once the site of the old Rockville Centre Institute. Being the tallest building at the time, the apartment building also provided a perfect precipice from which to search the sky for enemy planes.

In 1942, the United States Congress established a women's reserve to help the war effort by filling shore positions, freeing up officers and enlisted men for duty at sea. This new organization was known as the WAVES (Women Accepted for Volunteer Emergency Service). Among the women who joined was twenty-two-year-old Mildred LeViolette of Rockville Centre.

In the midst of all this war talk and preparedness, an amusing anecdote about Rockville Centre life occurred. On its way to join the circus, via Railway Express, a bear cub

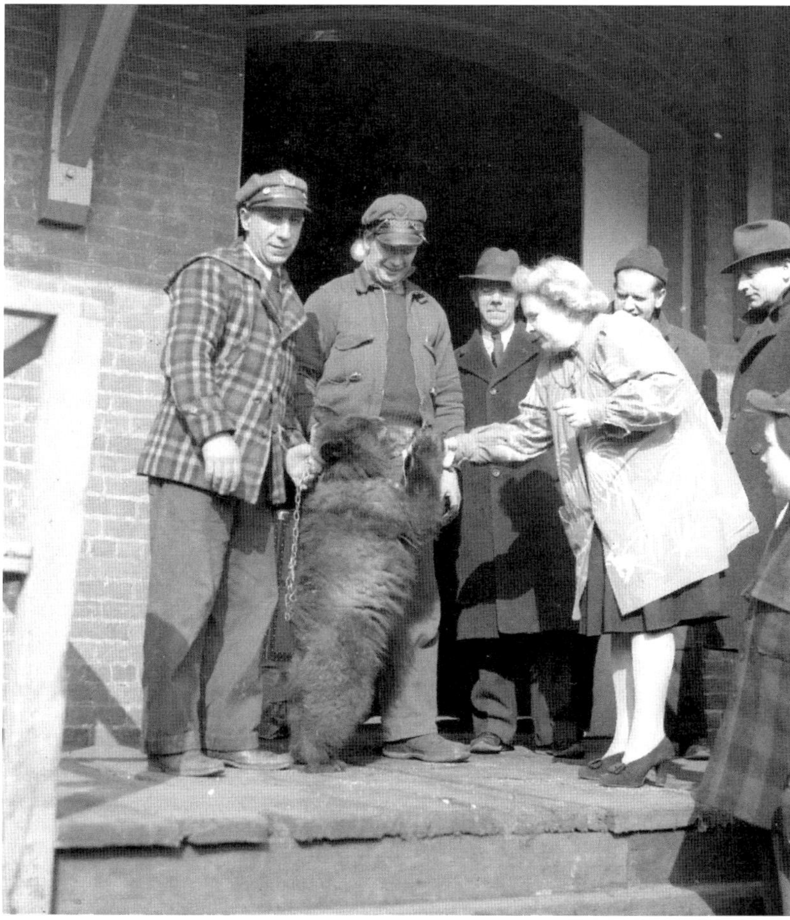

A bear cub being shipped via Railway Express was stranded in Rockville Centre in the winter of 1942, much to the delight of residents.

was stranded in the village. The cub was warmly welcomed and well taken care of by the residents. After several days, an upstate fire department came to the cub's rescue by adopting it.

Baseball would play a prominent role in the village's war bond drives and rallies. On August 26, 1942, a crowd of fifteen thousand turned out for a party and parade to raise money. Among the parade of two thousand uniformed marchers were New York Yankee greats Joe DiMaggio and Lefty Gomez.

In 1943, Bernard H. Lawson, president of the Rockville Centre Chamber of Commerce, was planning two other events for the war bond campaign. The first was a WNBC radio broadcast, hosted by Mary Margaret McBride, at South Side High School. The second event was "Rockville Centre Night at Ebbets Field," a twilight game between the New York Dodgers and the New York Giants. The highlight of the evening took place at a pre-game ceremony honoring Dixie Walker of the Dodgers, a member of the Rockville Centre Chamber of Commerce, and Bill Jurgis of the Giants, a Rockville Centre resident. Bernard H. Lawson presented both players with watches.

These events and the ongoing war bond sales brought in $1,500,000. The proceeds purchased eleven war planes, one of which was named the "Mayor of Rockville Centre" in honor of Mayor Walter J. Halliday, who interrupted his mayoral duties to join the United States Army.

A radio show on station WGBB called *Rockville Centre on the Air* was also sponsored by the chamber of commerce. It was a series of half-hour programs dedicated to the people of Rockville Centre. The show featured an interview with a serviceman or -woman of the week, a local organization of the week, musical entertainment and the latest news. William Kennedy, whose firm handled all of the village's public relations, was the host.

Throughout the war years, the Rockville Centre War Honor Roll Committee was hard at work keeping tabs on all the village's men and women serving around the world. One local resident who made the ultimate sacrifice was Second Lieutenant Raymond Seedorf, whose plane was shot down near Strasbourg, France, on April 22, 1945. Seedorf graduated from St. Agnes High School in 1941 and attended Niagara University before enlisting on December 8, 1942. He was the son of Mr. and Mrs.. Chauncy C. Seedorf of

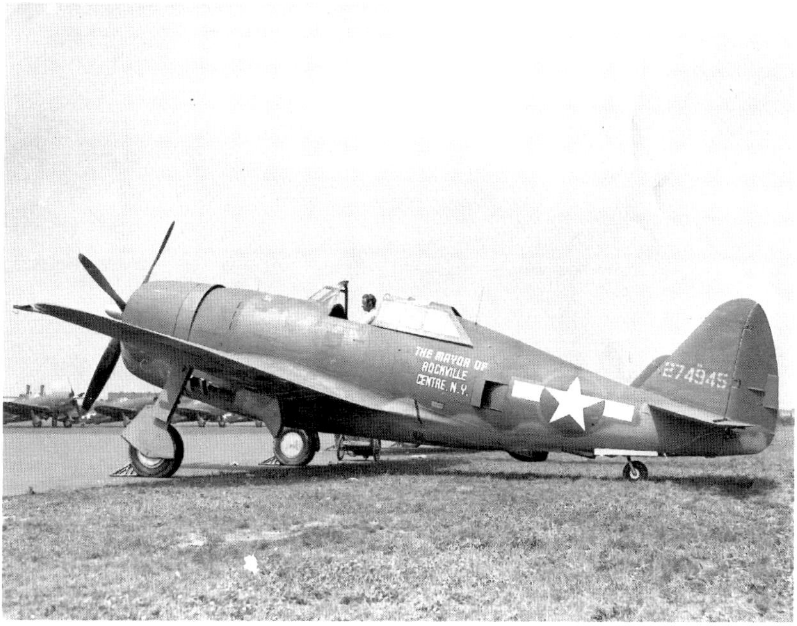

Several war planes were purchased through war bond drives held in Rockville Centre. One plane was named in honor of Mayor Walter J. Halliday.

Yale Place. Seedorf became one of many heroes when he shot down an enemy plane while a pilot in the Orange Tails Thunderbolt Fighter Squadron. He was the first pilot of his squadron to do so.

The War Honor Roll Committee published holiday greetings in the form of a newspaper to send to all the servicemen and -women serving in World War II. The paper kept them abreast of what was going on at home. It also carried columns on sports and entertainment contributed by the best newspaper writers and radio personalities of the day. In the 1944 edition, a notice appeared announcing that First Lady Eleanor Roosevelt would speak at a Democratic rally at South Side High School. In 1954, Roosevelt would again speak at the high school under the auspices of the congregation of Central Synagogue.

On Sunday, May 17, 1942, Edgar T. Beamish, mayor of Rockville Centre, dedicated the War Honor Roll Memorial at St. Agnes Field on Front Street. The dedication coincided with "I Am an American Day," proclaimed by President Franklin D. Roosevelt. The war memorial was later moved to the grounds of the John A. Anderson Recreation Center on Oceanside Road. The dedication took place on May 30, 1967. At the new War Memorial Plaza, a fountain from the 1964 World's Fair ground, purchased by the village, was installed by the Water Department.

The total number of Rockville Centre-ites who served in World War II was 3,130, and the total number of those who lost their lives was 74.

Chapter 6

BACK TO THE PRESENT

The 1950s brought an influx of veterans and their families to Rockville Centre, and the two major construction projects that had been put on hold during the Depression and World War II were progressing.

The elimination of the grade crossings by the Long Island Rail Road got underway when they put into service a single, temporary track to carry both east- and west-bound trains. Unfortunately, the project was further delayed when the engineer of an east-bound train ran a signal and crashed into a west-bound train. Thirty-three passengers were killed, and many more were injured, filling the local hospitals to overflowing. Rescue efforts continued through the night of February 17, 1950, and the people of Rockville Centre were again testing their mettle.

The project was completed on July 17, 1950, when the first Long Island Rail Road train to run on the overhead viaduct pulled into the station. On hand to celebrate with the residents of Rockville Centre was Thomas E. Dewey, then governor of New York State.

The second project to get underway was the alleviation of the traffic bottleneck where Merrick Road intersects with

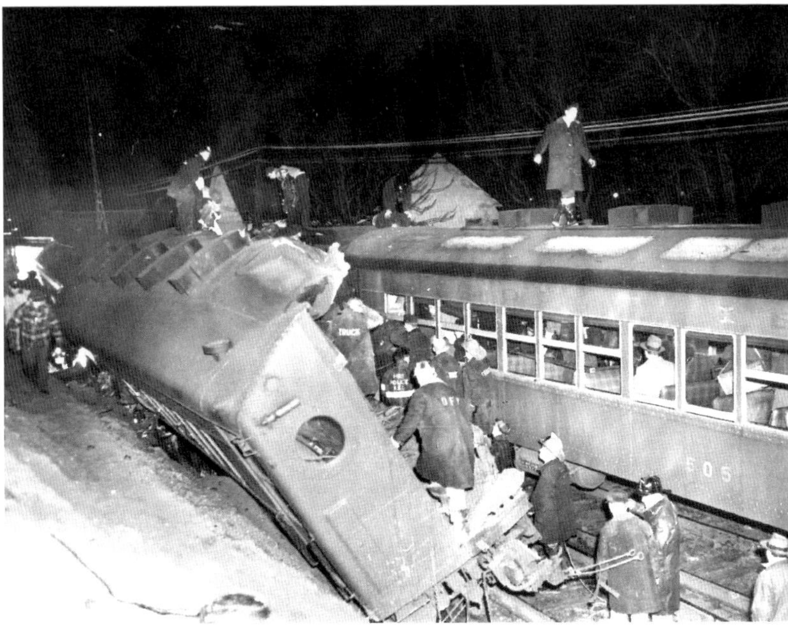

In 1950, during the Long Island Rail Road's elimination of grade crossings, two trains running on the same track collided head-on, killing thirty-three people.

Sunrise Highway. The original plans for what would become the Merrick-Sunrise Interchange were drawn up in the 1930s by W. Earle Andrews, a close friend of Long Island's master builder, Robert Moses, and a former assistant chief engineer of the Long Island State Park Commission. Completed in 1959, the interchange also alleviated the need for assigning four to seven policemen to direct traffic in the area.

Automobile traffic also increased, bringing more and more shoppers into the business district. A parking program was started with the development of the interiors of its business blocks into paved parking fields. Full-width street entrances were provided with adequate curbs and markings to maintain orderly use. Merchants improved the appearance of the rear of their stores, providing direct entrance from the new parking spaces.

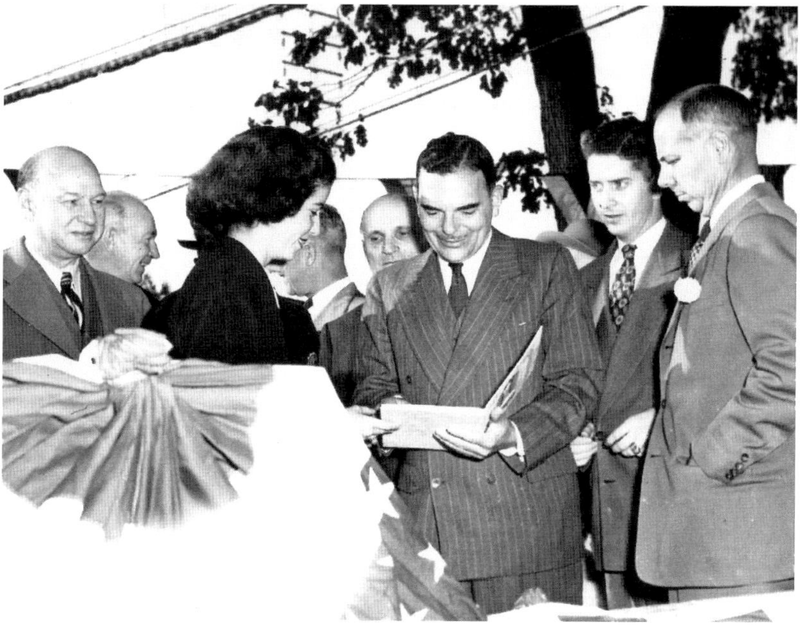

In 1950, the first train ran on the overhead viaduct, eliminating the street-level grade crossings. At the dedication ceremony was Governor Thomas E. Dewey.

Rockville Centre was running out of vacant land on which to build single-family homes in the residential neighborhoods. Throughout the 1950s and '60s, several apartment buildings sprang up. This trend continues today in the form of town houses, condos and the construction of a large apartment complex in the west end of the village. These are being built to accommodate the needs of older people looking to downsize and to keep the young people from moving out of Rockville Centre.

Sports were always a large part of village life, and in the mid-'50s, it became apparent that the combination of village funds and school facilities was no longer meeting the needs of this, once again, growing village. In 1955, the village created a Department of Recreation and opened a temporary center in the newly built Water Department storage warehouse and garage on Maple Avenue. The residents' response was immediate and enthusiastic, and soon both indoor and outdoor recreational programs were greatly expanded.

With the success of the temporary center, plans were initiated for a permanent home. The village purchased from the City of New York thirteen acres that had once been the site of the Brooklyn Water Works Dry Reservoir and the Rockville Centre Airport. On three acres of this repurposed site, the John A. Anderson Recreation Center and Children's Playground was built. Opening in 1960, it housed an auditorium, multipurpose room, large gymnasium, entrance hall and lounge. There were also an arts and crafts room, a kitchen, a wrestling room, a rifle and pistol range, a large-table game room, offices, a utility room, showers and locker rooms.

Many years later, the building was demolished, and a new, more modern building took its place. Today, more than three hundred popular programs, classes and activities for residents of all ages are available at the John A. Anderson Recreation Center/Anthony T. Brunetta Pavilion on North Oceanside Road, as well as at the Martin Luther King Jr. Community Center on Centre Avenue. The Recreation Department also oversees and schedules the use of all parks and fields. Popular sports include soccer, lacrosse, women's softball, baseball and basketball.

A great honor was bestowed on Rockville Centre thanks to the extraordinary vision of Monsignor Peter Quealy. St. Agnes Parish became the seat of the diocese of Rockville Centre. On April 18, 1957, Pope Pius XII separated the counties of Nassau and Suffolk from the diocese of Brooklyn, making Rockville Centre an Episcopal city and St. Agnes Church a cathedral.

On May 26, 1957, the Most Reverend Walter P. Kellenburg, DD, arrived at the Nassau County line, where he was met by a parade of welcomers to escort him to St. Agnes. Upon arrival, Kellenburg was ordained as the first bishop of the diocese of Rockville Centre. After a brief period of prayer,

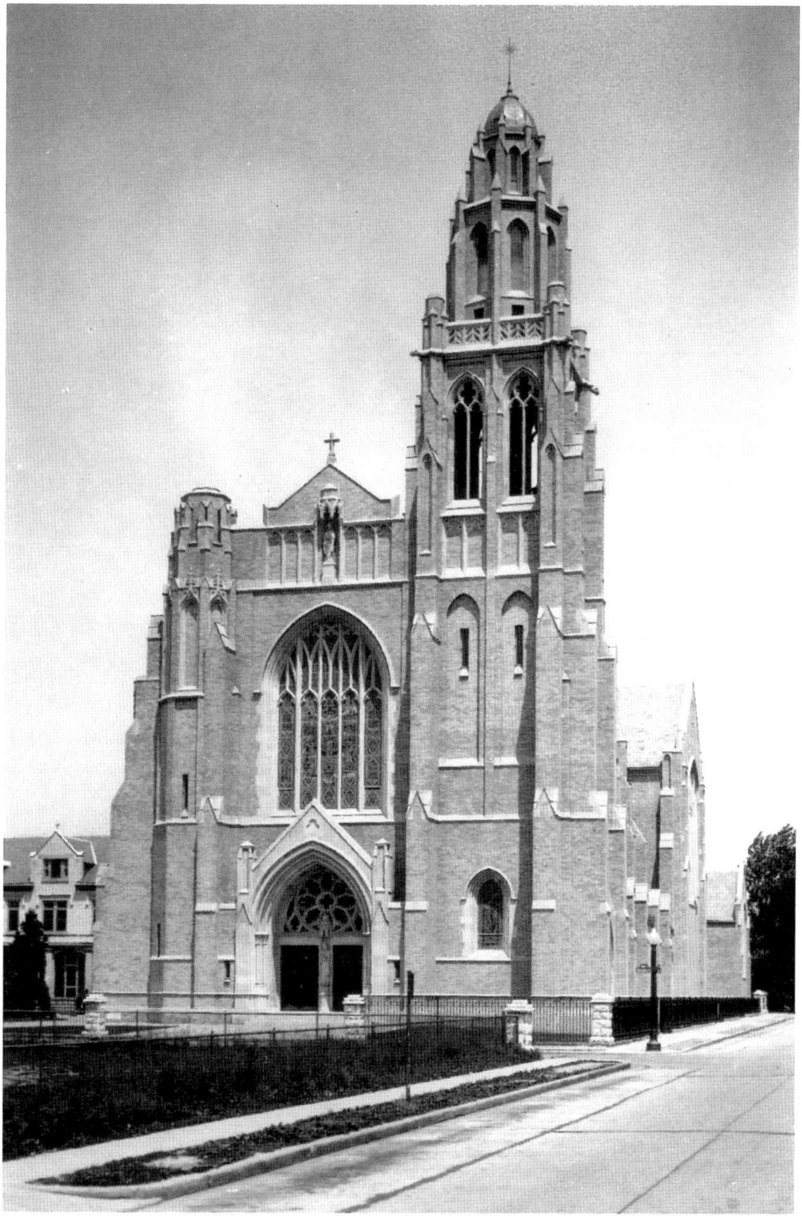

St. Agnes Cathedral, built under the supervision of Monsignor Peter Quealy, became the centerpiece of the diocese of Rockville Centre in 1957.

Bishop Kellenburg proceeded to the reviewing stand at the corner of Clinton Avenue and Front Street, where he was joined by village officials. Bishop Kellenburg then blessed the large crowd of well-wishers and parade participants.

Also during the 1950s, the American Broadcasting Company's station WJZ-TV designated Monday, March 10, 1952, Rockville Centre Day. Mayor W. Harry Lister was asked to invite a group of village officials and about forty women from the village to participate in interviews, quizzes and contests on the popular television program *Club Matinee*. A pre-program luncheon was held at Healy's Restaurant at 66th Street and Columbus Avenue in New York City.

In 1952, village residents passed a $2.6 million bond issue for construction of the third building to become South Side High School. Groundbreaking began on December 8, 1953, and the cornerstone was placed in October 1954. Designed to house one thousand students in grades ten through twelve, the new high school opened on September 15, 1955. In 1982, an addition was opened to accommodate the ninth-grade students. The school is proud of its high percentage of college-bound graduates and its many modern facilities.

Three days earlier, on September 12, 1955, the Dominican sisters opened Molloy Catholic College for Women. The first class of forty-four freshmen convened classes in an unused mansion at 915 North Village Avenue. The college, which has been coed since 1982, now stands at 1000 Hempstead Avenue. It has one of the largest and finest nursing programs in the country. The college also has extensive continuing education programs.

Plans for an urban renewal program slated for the west end of the village, one of the first areas of settlement in Rockville Centre, were announced in 1955. The plans were delayed for ten years due to the contentiousness, miscommunication and disagreements between the village board and the residents about what was allowed to become a rundown, unsafe, blighted area.

On October 7, 1965, the final plans for urban renewal in the west end were formally approved by the village board. Eventually, nine multiple-use dwellings were built, providing 164 moderate- to middle-income apartments on North Centre Avenue just south of Maine Avenue. Mr. and Mrs. Edward Lloyd and their nineteen-year-old son, Steven, made history when they became the first family to move into the apartment complex.

Today, the complex, which has recently been completely renovated, operates under the Rockville Centre Housing Authority's seven-member board of commissioners and has a very capable director and office staff. The housing authority also operates a fifty-unit apartment building on Merrick Road, affectionately known as the Senior Building.

On March 26, 1968, the Reverend Martin Luther King Jr. spoke to a standing-room-only audience at South Side Junior High School in Rockville Centre on his vision for the civil rights movement. Nine days later, King was struck down by an assassin's bullet in Memphis, Tennessee. One year later, on March 26, 1969, a musical tribute to Reverend Martin Luther King Jr. was held in the junior high school. The tribute was organized by the former Rockville Centre Chapter of the Poor People's Campaign, which had only recently become an affiliate of the Southern Christian Leadership Conference, an organization King helped to create.

In 1971, the Rockville Centre United Presbyterian Church and the Congregational Church of Rockville Centre combined their two congregations under the leadership of their respective pastors, Reverend Harry T. Mathias and Reverend Richard W. Lund. For a time, they worshipped by alternating between the two churches. Eventually changing their name to the United Church of Rockville Centre, they began holding all services at the former Congregational church on Morris Avenue between Hamilton and Princeton Streets.

In the mid-1970s, our nation was celebrating its bicentennial, and Rockville Centre's residents were busy with their own celebratory plans. An American Revolution Bicentennial Committee was taking the lead under the aegis of village trustee Frederick P. Cole. Several subcommittees were formed to ensure that everyone in the village would be included. Dorothy Prink Cancelliere, village historian, chaired the Heritage Committee; Helen Kraus chaired the Festival Committee; Robert C. Williams and Eugene Yourch headed the Horizon Committee; Rose Roden Silvers coordinated the School-College-Religious effort; and George L. Shibler handled all the public relations.

A gala colonial fête took place at Molloy College on November 30, 1975. Guests in colonial garb were greeted by Minutemen, and a colonial fife and drum corps provided the entertainment. A well-organized parade on July 3, 1976, kicked off a weeklong celebration. The whole village turned out to view the many organizations that had built their own parade floats. Also represented were the police department, fire department, schools, Scout troops and many others too numerous to count. To round out the day, a country fair, picnic and fireworks display took place as an after party.

July 4, 1976, was the most anticipated event of the bicentennial celebration. Not only was Rockville Centre celebrating its own HERitage and HIStory, it was also taking part in the larger celebration of our nation. It was a time of great reflection that sparked a surge among small towns and villages everywhere to retrieve and preserve their own past, saving it for future generations. The most enduring legacy to come out of Rockville Centre's bicentennial celebration was the preservation of the Captain Samuel F. Phillips House, now the Museum of the Village of Rockville Centre.

After thirty-three years, the museum was finally granted its absolute charter on December 15, 2009, by the New York State Board of Regents. Not only has the museum grown in stature, through the efforts of the many volunteer members of the museum's board of trustees, both past and present, but it has also grown into one of the finest small museums on Long Island. The museum's many permanent and

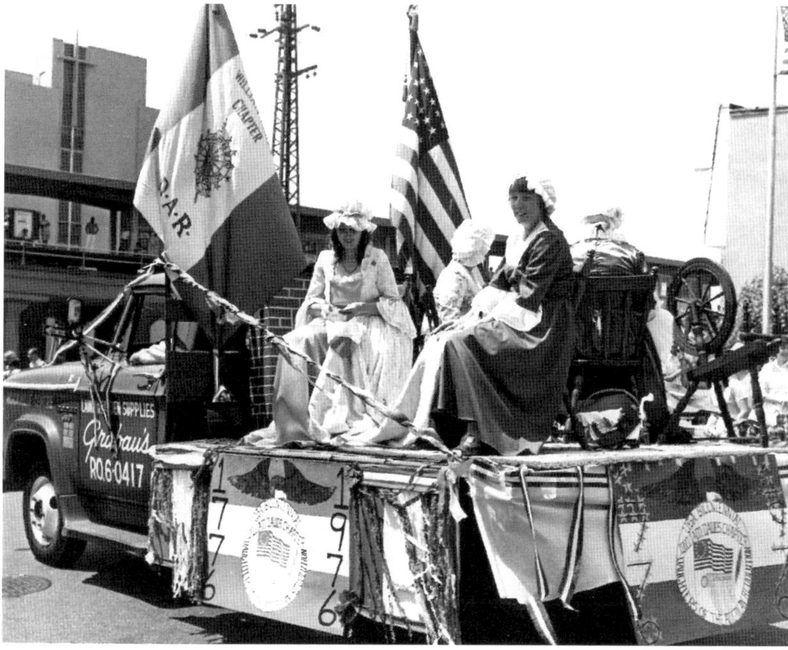

The women of the William E. Dawes Chapter of the Daughters of the American Revolution's float in Rockville Centre's bicentennial parade in 1976.

temporary exhibits draw people from all over and also draw the attention of the press, which includes the museum in its events calendars and feature articles. People are also drawn to the museum's beautiful gardens, which provide them with a quiet place. The museum also houses an extensive historic archive available to anyone interested in learning more about Rockville Centre's past and present.

Hopefully, this narrative will help those who read it to take away the lessons to be learned from the past and to gain the wisdom of the pioneering, progressive people who helped make Rockville Centre not only a great place to live, but a wonderful way of life as well. They are the role models of the future.

INDEX

ABOUT THE AUTHOR

Marilyn Nunes Devlin was a trustee and is currently a volunteer archivist at the Museum of Rockville Centre, where she has been active in designing exhibits, fundraising, making policy and working as a docent for many years. She has resided in Rockville Centre for thirty-five years, during which time she has been active in community service and a member of the Fortnightly Club, a women's organization founded in 1898. She has also worked as the editor of the Friends of the Rockville Centre Library's newsletter and has served as a member of the Board of Trustees of the Rockville Centre Library for ten years.